BLOOD
&
GHOSTS

Paranormal Forensics Investigators

D1525380

by

Mark Nesbitt

&

Katherine Ramsland

Published by   Second Chance Publications
P.O. Box 3126
Gettysburg, PA. 17325

ISBN 10: 0-9849063-6-3
ISBN 13: 978-0-9849063-6-9

Photos by authors or are public domain unless otherwise credited.
Original cover design by Carol Nesbitt

Table of Contents

Introduction

It started with a ghost story. It ended with a full forensic investigation. The following tale illustrates how we envision coordinating crime-solving tools with paranormal phenomena. Sometimes a paranormal event, like the one described below, triggers an investigation, and sometimes an investigation, such as a missing person case, seeks a paranormal solution. Hence, the idea of paranormal forensics. We'll describe a range of ways these two approaches to crime can be used together. So, back to the ghost story.

"Duffy's Cut" is a stretch of railroad track at Mile 59 near Malvern, PA, about thirty miles west of Philadelphia. It was built in 1832 for the Philadelphia and Columbia Railroad, which later became part of the Pennsylvania system. Mile 59 was a particularly difficult stretch. To make the land level for a track, a hill had to be dug out and the dirt used to fill a neighboring ravine.

Contractor Philip Duffy hired fifty-seven of his fellow Irishmen straight off the docks to work on this difficult task. Setting up in a camp, they had to cut their way through dense woods, heavy soil, and rocky terrain. Soon, some contracted cholera, a contagious and deadly disease that had become pandemic throughout the world. Because they were poor Irish Catholic immigrants, against whom there was rampant prejudice, they received little to no medical care. Industry owners viewed them as expendable.

Three perished quickly and Duffy's blacksmith buried them in individual graves. But then more died. By some reports, it was eight or nine, but a letter from a railroad administrator indicated that half of Duffy's crew had been wiped out. Within two months of starting on this job, they were all dead.

A ditch was dug for the rest of the bodies, not far from the tracks where they'd been making the fill. No death certificates were completed or properly filed. No families back in Ireland were notified. These men were considered anonymous beings who deserved nothing better. Official records went into the railroad's vaults, marked confidential.

In 1909, an investigation inspired the collection of numerous files, including the records of the 1832 cholera outbreak that had swept through the camp. Pennsylvania Railroad President Martin Clermont concluded at this time that, despite a lack of supporting evidence, all fifty-seven men had perished from the disease.

When the company went bankrupt, Joseph Tripician, Clermont's personal secretary, removed the files from Clermont's safe and stored them in his home. After Tripician's death, his grandson, Reverend Frank Watson, a religious historian, discovered them. Their confidential status intrigued him.

With his twin brother, Dr. William "Bill" Watson, a history professor at Immaculata University, Frank researched the case. Saddened by the way the men had been buried and forgotten, the brothers placed a historical marker near the site of the mass grave. But they remained curious.

They had heard their grandfather tell ghost stories about the area. The file included a report from a man walking home along the tracks on a warm September night, who claimed to have seen blue and green lights dancing on the mass grave.

Many people believe that ghosts are restless souls, unable to find peace because of something that occurred regarding their deaths. This story, along with the file's confidentiality and the fact that cholera should not have wiped out the entire camp, inspired the brothers to get more involved. They knew the approximate location of the camp, so in 2004, despite their lack of archaeological experience, they started digging. At the same time they also examined diaries, books, and newspaper accounts. Among the hundreds of artifacts they dug up were eating utensils, remnants of a shanty, glass buttons, and a pipe sporting an Irish logo.

Bill invited a forensic anthropologist, Janet Monge, and geophysicist, Tim Bechtel, to assist in the Duffy's Cut Project. Bechtel performed an x-ray scan of the earth with ground-penetrating radar and found suggestive anomalies—large pockets of air perhaps left behind by decomposing bodies. This was the first indication that they might actually locate the remains of the long-dead workers. It was near where the original track had been laid.

It took a while, and a lot of digging, but on March 20, 2009, the team made a startling discovery: a human bone. This led to unearthing a skull. Soon they found a couple more. One skull was perforated by what resembled a bullet hole, and lead residue on the hole's rim confirmed it. Two other skulls appear to have been bashed with a blunt object, or slashed with an axe blade.

A newspaper account from October 3, 1832, detailed the cholera outbreak, and stated that several men tried to leave to avoid getting sick. However, families who lived nearby refused to assist and agents for their employer forced them into quarantine. The Watsons surmised that area residents, panicking over the possibility of contracting the disease, came into the camp and killed these men.

As of 2010, they had found the remains of five men and a woman, but just four skulls. "All of the remains found so far," William stated to a reporter, "indicate that the men were brutally murdered."

One set of remains was that of an adolescent. His skull bones were not yet fused, which helped to establish his approximate age. An x-ray revealed that he had not grown a right upper molar, a genetic defect that could assist to identify him. The team found a record of John Ruddy, an 18-year-old who had sailed from Derry, Ireland, on the only ship in the spring of 1832 going to Philadelphia.

Word of this discovery reached Ireland, and a Ruddy family from Donegal contacted the Watsons. Some of them had the same dental defect. Ruddy's identity was confirmed by comparing the size of his bones to measurements on the ship's manifest, so even before the results of a DNA analysis were complete, his remains were sent to Ireland for burial among his kin.

The other victims were properly buried on March 9, 2012, under a Celtic cross in West Laurel Hill Cemetery, among people who once looked down on them. The Watsons believed they have just begun to find the Duffy's Cut victims. They suspected there is a mass grave near their archeological dig, containing at least 50 more bodies. They had hoped to continue the project, but Amtrak said the grave was too close to active tracks and denied the exhumation request.

Ghost Science

During the 1840s, as the scientific method became the dominant means for gathering knowledge, ghost tales and spiritualism were drawing huge crowds to celebrity mediums who claimed to have privileged contact with the dead. Scientists, embracing the physical world, dismissed them out of hand, and teams of investigators set out to prove the impossibility of a paranormal force.

However, a select few decided to give it a fair hearing, hoping to bring the same investigative methods to "spiritism" that they applied to other subjects. In fact, Italian anthropologist Cesare Lombroso, who focused on the criminal mind, was the first person on record to devise a form of paranormal forensics. You'll read more about him in a later chapter. During his era, criminologists believed they had a talent for perceiving the invisible forces of a personality. Their founding attitude was curiosity, an open mind, and the desire to gain knowledge with solid investigative methods. This attitude sets the standard to which this book, *Blood & Ghosts*, aspires.

One of us coined the term, "ghosting," in *Ghost: Investigating the Other Side*, to describe the many activities associated with ghosts. There are people who merely collect the lore, locally, nationally, or internationally, while others strive to spot or photograph a ghost. They might also seek to record ghostly voices, research the story behind a haunting, or ask a psychic for help. Perhaps they'll conduct a séance to try to communicate. Or they might believe that a ghost must be exorcised, so they'll do things like burn sage or ask a priest or medium to cleanse the place. All of these activities come under the idea of ghosting. But for us, it's mostly about investigating and documenting actual events related to what we've heard about or recorded.

The well-equipped ghost hunter relies largely on digital and other types of technology. There are basically four types of ghost hunting equipment: Detecting, recording, communicating, and analyzing.

First, it must be said that there is no such thing as a "ghost detector." The only things we can detect are anomalies—an electromagnetic spike in the middle of an open field where there are no man-made electromagnetic sources; a drop in temperature in a room where there is no air-conditioning or draft. To detect these anomalies we utilize electromagnetic field (EMF) meters and quick-read thermometers. We typically carry a digital camera, and a video recorder with infrared lighting for night (or an infrared filter for photographs taken during the daytime) to record anything that is detected. Voice recorders (digital or tape) help with communicating by collecting electronic voice phenomena (EVP—the alleged voices of the dead, unheard except on electronic devices). Sometimes dowsing rods and pendulums are used to communicate as well.

We're familiar with computer software that enhances photographs and recordings.

Some paranormal investigators utilize more sophisticated equipment such as heat sensing video recorders. Others prefer to present the "human side" forward and ask sensitives—mediums, or psychics—to participate and relate names they receive psychically for use in communication, which are then documented by the scientific equipment.

Examples of Paranormal Investigation Equipment

The five basic types of manifestations on photos are the following: bright round light anomalies referred to as "orbs" (usually white but multi-colored as well); a string of those, which form a vortex; a long, electrical snakelike image (or group of images); foggy stuff that we call ectoplasm or paranormal mist; and the rare but exciting apparition. This can take the form of a single body part, such as a hand, a head or pair of legs, or it can be the entire image of a person. It might be transparent or solid, in color or all white. It might even be a dark shadow. Of all these anomalies, orbs are the most controversial.

Paranormal Mist & Orbs

Often people will take photos in the snow or rain, or when the air is filled with dust. If they happen to be at a haunted site, they are certain the scores of white, transparent, circular images are spirits when all they've caught are extreme close-ups of suspended particles. And yet there are the videos of orbs rushing toward the camera and dodging it, or moving to and fro upon request, or passing through solid objects, something dust has yet been unable to do. Orbs continue to be a mysterious part of the paranormal.

Similar to the days of spiritualism, ghost hunting is plagued by superstition, fraud, and wishful thinking. There are those who take it seriously, but there are many who seek merely to exploit it. Although there have been many attempts throughout the decades to apply the scientific method to ghostly incidents, few investigators have spotted the value of using forensic science to test alleged manifestations. Even fewer realize that paranormal investigations, if done well, might aid the cause of justice.

Inside these pages, we'll examine tales of ghosts and murder, police psychics, and scientific experiments. We'll also pose a challenge: what if forensic and paranormal investigation deliberately crossed paths? Can forensics aid ghost hunters, and might ghost hunters who use these tools one day assist in the cause of justice?

Paranormalist Mark Nesbitt, author of the popular *Ghosts of Gettysburg* series, and Katherine Ramsland, author of *Beating the Devil's Game: A History of Forensic Science and Criminal Investigation* and *The Forensic Science of CSI*, combine these two disciplines. Mark has experience with paranormal investigations, while Katherine knows about forensic science and investigation. She has also worked with coroners and profilers.

We met ten years ago when Katherine was writing *Ghost: Investigating the Other Side*. Mark was running ghost tours in Gettysburg and documenting the many sightings of paranormal phenomena in the area. He had just started to participate in investigations, and his own office in Gettysburg ("The Ghost House") turned out to be haunted. Once a park ranger, after five years, Mark quit the Park Service to research and write. In addition to several historical accounts of the Civil War, he wrote seven volumes of the *Ghosts of Gettysburg* series based on stories sent to him, as well as field guides for paranormal investigators.

Long-time partners in paranormal research, Katherine and Mark apply different perspectives to exploring the phenomena. In fact, Katherine has been nicknamed "Bones," due to her stubborn insistence on evidence for claims and on interpretations that make logical sense.

Around the time we met, Katherine was learning to use infrared and digital technology to capture images and ethereal voices. We set up several experiments together. Neither of us expected to get much, but we were willing to try.

At dusk one brisk evening in December, we trekked out to a site on the Gettysburg battlefield known as the Triangular Field, near Devil's Den. Named before the Civil War, Devil's Den is a maze of large boulders that proved perfect cover for sharpshooters. Given its location near Little Round Top, where the Yankees had gained the high ground, Confederate soldiers used the rocks to maintain a barrage of fire.

Nearby is a creek called Bloody Run, which was said to have turned red from all the blood that ran from soldiers being shot during the intense battle that ensued here. Across the road from Devil's Den is the Triangular Field. Soldiers from Georgia and Texas had fought their way across this field, and many had fallen, lying in agony from the shrapnel and minié balls that shattered their flesh and bones. At least one theory holds that an expenditure of intense emotion is what allows supernatural energy to be trapped in ghostly form, and we had plenty of that in this very tight space: anger, fear, agony, desperation, determination, and courage.

Mark had a list of the names of men who had served in the various regiments in the Triangular Field. He didn't know how many from this list had actually died there, but his plan was to call the roll as if he were an officer. As darkness gathered, Katherine would be filming it with infrared light. Until then, she would use a digital camera for still shots. We knew that many people had experienced disabled camera equipment in this place, so we were prepared for the worst. We'd brought plenty of fresh batteries.

Triangular Field in Gettysburg, Pennsylvania

Mark turned on a digital recorder and reeled off a few names, while Katherine snapped shots. She captured an orb not far from him—a ball of light that many people interpret as a ghost. When we played the recorder back, we listened to Mark calling out names. After one, we heard a distinct male response, "Yessir!" Even

"Bones" had to admit that this was a voice beyond the physical world. So, this was the start of the partnership that led to this book.

We'll begin with our historical mentors who thought that the scientific investigation of criminals and crime could be applied to the investigation of paranormal events. Then we'll show how such investigations are done today.

It seems that certain violent incidents have left an aura— fleeting telltale odors, cold spots, nudges, noises, or wispy apparitions, sometimes lingering for decades, even centuries. While not all haunted sites are about murder, that's what we're most concerned with. Murders or ambiguous deaths launch forensic investigations, so we then have a basis into which to insert paranormal methods and ideas. We're interested in where forensics and paranormal approaches come together to mutually assist each other.

Katherine & Mark Investigating Andersonville Prison

Paranormal theories emerge from data patterns where apparent hauntings occur: for example, some theories hold that ghosts are spawned in the wake of an untimely or sudden death, or from an urgent need to finish unfulfilled earthly duties. Ghost hunters today believe that with the latest cutting-edge technology they can access the Other Side to shed light on both active and unsolved cold cases, and many believe that murder victims linger to see justice done.

Ghost hunters have devised many techniques for capturing this data, but few have looked into the cache of current and future forensic tools for ideas.

Forensics is an applied science and many of its sub-disciplines have a kinship with ghost hunting: its tools and technology were devised to record and analyze evidence or behavior. Given this shared approach to solving mysteries, it makes sense to see how we can bring these disciplines together. From missing persons to mass and serial murder, it's time to use all of our best resources.

Katherine co-wrote a book with Gregg McCrary, a former F.B.I. Supervisory Special Agent and a member of the famed Behavioral Science Unit (BSU, but now known as the BAU), about his cases. Called *The Unknown Darkness*, it described the psychological nature of criminal investigation. We asked Gregg to comment on some of the investigative aspects of paranormal forensics, and he agreed. In fact, one of the cases involved him, which we detail in a later chapter.

Because we've worked together and apart, our approach for this book is this: when just one of us is involved, we'll alert you to who will be taking you into this realm. When it's both, we'll speak as a team. As we offer tips from (and for) both sides, we will detail the factual background and paranormal events involved in some of the most chilling ghost—and murder—stories ever told.

Scientists and Séances

George Pellew (to whom researchers gave the pseudonym "Pelham"), 32, was a promising philosopher. During the 1890s, he befriended Richard Hodgson, a member of the American Society for Psychical Research. At the time, Hodgson was investigating a quirky but talented medium named Leonora Piper, and Pelham sometimes went with him.

Leonora Piper

Pelham listened to Hodgson's ideas about the continuation of the soul after death, but remained skeptical. He found the concept of a spirit existence absurd, but he jokingly promised that if he died first and if Hodgson and his colleagues were correct, he would return to affirm it. In fact, he vowed, he would make such an obvious appearance no one could deny it. If the spirit world is real, he said, he would prove it. However, he did not expect to get this opportunity so quickly.

While riding through Central Park during the winter of 1892, Pelham was killed when his horse slipped on a patch of ice. Hodgson mourned the loss of his friend, but wondered if Pelham's ghost might now make an appearance. He continued to monitor Mrs. Piper, and now he had a keenly personal interest.

At first, there was no evidence that the young philosopher was going to show. But a month after Pelham's death, Mrs. Piper channeled an entity who introduced himself via her regular spirit guide as Pelham, or G. P.

Hodgson was astonished, but not ready to call this proof of the afterlife. He put the claim to every scientific test he could think of. To discount the possibility of telepathy, Hodgson invited Pelham's former friends and relatives to come anonymously and ask questions they believed the medium could never guess. He also brought people there who did not know Pelham at all.

To the strangers (the controls), G. P. had nothing to say. To friends and relatives, he offered detailed and accurate answers that satisfied them. In fact, G. P. spoke to them all in the manner he would have used had he been alive, albeit through automatic writing. One man kept a message, which was several pages long, to himself, but assured Hodgson that he was satisfied that the spirit G. P. was Pelham.

This untimely death in Central Park, Hodgson believed, offered one of the few compelling demonstrations of the possibility of life after death. It is also one of the earliest attempts to test spirit activity with science. Piper was never exposed as a fraud, and quite a few people reportedly carried on conversations with Pelham after death. We discussed the case with Gregg McCrary, who had done forensic analysis of handwriting samples.

"I think they should have done handwriting analysis," Katherine said.

"But that wouldn't discount him if it doesn't match," Mark pointed out.

Gregg agreed. Mark and Gregg both thought the syntax should be consistent, and should show the idiosyncrasies. Gregg recalled working a case that had required the analysis of a ransom note for a kidnapped CEO, Sidney Reso. The tone of the letter had had a terroristic edge. The authors had signed it "Rainbow Warriors," but the team thought this was a deflection. As the communications continued, they'd seen a revealing tone and psychological pattern. They'd concluded that the letter was from a Yuppie couple in Morristown. This came from the tone and surrounding items that revealed their identities. Based on dog hairs found in the letter, it was also determined that the couple owned a Golden Retriever.

"You'd be looking for the use of language that was characteristic of the author," Gregg said. "People can't help who they are. It leaks out. The linguistics should be from the culture, the era, and something about him."

We agreed that Hodgson seemed to have done a lot of good investigating of other aspects, and that an analysis of the linguistic characteristics of the communication would have just added a layer.

Yet, scientists had tried and failed to expose the Fox sisters, who'd created a worldwide movement, spiritualism, in response to a murder case. Their confessions years after they became celebrities revealed their devious tricks.

Today, the debate continues. Despite Pelham's seemingly remarkable appearance, there are few other such documented incidents. In fact, despite pushing through from the Other Side and also being a philosopher, he doesn't seem to have resolved any of the big questions about the spirit world. His various appearances were mostly limited to mundane chit-chats, which hardly seems "proof" from a man intent on showing Hodgson something worth documenting. He did describe the difficulties of spirit communication and said that entering the discarnate world was jarring and confusing at first. However, few ghost hunters today even know about him. He hardly made a splash.

Although many groups claim to be verifying their findings with the scientific method, fraud is still rife and quite a few participants have the wrong idea about what scientific testing requires.

The Scientific Method

Scientific knowledge is acquired from relying on systematic, objective observation to make deductions and create formulas from physical laws, as well as testing those deductions through articulated hypotheses and controlled experiments that afford replicable results. You might then continue to observe the patterns under more controlled conditions and perhaps note that your initial observations were in error. The point is to try to *disprove* a hypothesis, not to prove it. When you try the latter, you become vulnerable to confirmation bias: seeing what you want to see. Anyone can prove a hypothesis by bending the facts to fit. It's not nearly as easy to disprove a hypothesis. If it can't be done, then you have a solid hypothesis upon which to start building a theory.

Once you have some patterns established (and also lack patterns that contradict it), you can proceed with a more controlled approach. If your experiment can't be brought into the lab to control for all possible variables, you must try out your ideas in different circumstances and settings, with other variables (different weather conditions, inside or outdoors, different temperatures, different lighting effects, etc.). It may also serve your purposes to have other people—ignorant of your results—make observations to get objective agreement. Thus, we might approach our subject, the paranormal, in order to accomplish any of several things:

• Determine causes of certain actions.
• Eliminate all possible explanations but one.
• Conceptualize a core essence.
• Define specific situations in which the activity occurs.
• Predict future occurrences.

So, now that we have a sense of science, what about forensic science?

The Science of Crime

Crime scene analysis is a combination of criminalistics and criminology. Criminalistics is the application of science to physical items, such as bloodstains, soil, saliva, and bullet trajectories. Criminology is the psychological angle, which involves studying crime scenes for motives, traits, and behavior, which will help to interpret the evidence.

For example, when tread from the tire on a woman's car matches the tread pattern left at the scene of a hit-and-run, criminalistics can link her to the incident. However, when her denial rings false, ideas about reading deception in behavior come from criminology, and the investigator then takes the case further to see what the woman is hiding. Some psychology is always at play in the recreation of a criminal event.

Forensics is an applied science and many of its sub-disciplines have a kinship with ghost hunting: its tools and technology record, crystallize, and analyze evidence. As well, in the past decade, experienced ghost hunters have become more rigorous in their investigative methodology, and some have used innovative instruments to detect, capture, and analyze events that occur at a haunted site. Given this shared approach to solving mysteries, it makes sense to see what each discipline offers the other.

The Nature of Evidence

Death investigations rely on all types of evidence, the more the better. There are two basic kinds of evidence: testimonial and physical. Testimonial comes from anyone who was near a scene and saw something. Detectives can use the information to help obtain search warrants or develop leads.

1. Physical evidence is grouped into one of five categories:
2. Temporary (may change or be lost)
3. Conditional (associated with specific conditions at the crime scene)
4. Associative (links a suspect or victim to a scene)
5. Pattern (blood, impressions, tire treads, residue or evidence of the modus operandi)
6. Trace/transfer (produced by physical contact with some surface).

Similarly, ghost hunting utilizes witness reports and physical evidence collected by various devices to help understand a paranormal incident. Some also add "psychic evidence." Many paranormalists could benefit from specific instruments or skills developed in the forensic arena.

First Forensic Paranormalists

The 19th century saw the emergence of the scientific method as the dominant means for acquiring knowledge about the world. The scientific establishment denounced "ignorant" spiritualists who claimed that there existed paranormal forces all around us. However, a few scientists decided that an open mind was the basis for all science, so they opted to attend spiritualist sessions.

Among them were American psychologist William James, British philosopher Henry Sidgwick, and Italian criminologist Cesare Lombroso. In fact, Lombroso was instrumental in founding early theories of criminology, so let's first look at his contribution. It formed the basis for his approach to spirits.

In 1876, Cesare Lombroso published a slim volume about his work in criminal anthropology, which grew through successive editions into the classic multi-volume study *L'uomo delinquent* (*The Criminal Man*). He'd made systematic measurements of the body parts of numerous offenders to develop his notion that criminality was inherited, and its propensity was apparent in the body's physical appearance. Unlike normal people, the "born criminal" was genetically defective.

Although Lombroso's ideas have long been discredited, he was instrumental in shifting the study of criminal behavior into the realm of science. He founded the Italian School of Positivist Criminology, worked on a rudimentary lie detector, and advocated for a cautious approach to the death penalty.

Cesare Lombroso

Not particularly tidy, his workspace resembled a junkyard, yet out of this chaos he established one of the earliest professional museums dedicated to crime. He watched for other consistent clues of character as he collected skulls, skeletons, brains, and objects associated with lunatics and criminals. When he became a professor of psychiatry at the University of Pavia, his publications attracted professionals across Europe who were interested in anthropology. To support and assist him, many sent him crime-related items from their institutions.

"Our theories," Lombroso wrote, "are based on a mass of facts that are there for all to see; it has proved that despite the opposition from distinguished men, our school has attracted and convinced the best scientists in Europe who did not disdain to send us…the most valuable documents in their collection."

In 1908, the New York *World* asked Lombroso to comment on a singularly shocking case of an American serial killer—a woman. Her tale is also part of ghost lore today, so we should take a brief detour before we return to Lombroso's ideas on ghosts.

The Mystery of Belle Gunness

A fire on April 28 gutted the La Porte, Indiana, farmhouse of Belle Gunness, a Norwegian-American widow. Reportedly, she was inside with her daughter and two sons, and once the fire was extinguished, four corpses were found in the charred ruins. At first no one doubted that the adult corpse was Belle, although the figure was smaller than the six-foot pig farmer…and missing its head. The fire had been intentionally set and the prime suspect, former hired hand Ray Lamphere, was arrested.

As the embers cooled, investigators searched the property for the remains of a man named Andrew Helgelein (or Helgelien, on the gravestone), who'd been missing for the past three months. Belle had written letters imploring him to sell everything he had and come to her, and afterward no one heard from him. His brother had insisted on a full investigation. Not long afterward, Belle's house burned down.

From a freshly filled hole on the pig farm, the authorities turned up a stinking gunnysack. Inside were the dismembered parts of the missing man. His legs had been sawed off above the knees, his arms disarticulated, and his head removed.

Then diggers found another soft spot in the ground nearby. This one yielded the skeletal remains of a girl, and more digging turned up the decayed remains of a man and two children.

The area became a massive crime scene, and before it was over, the authorities had pulled out an estimated twelve to thirteen sets of remains, mostly male. They wondered if Belle, a woman, could possibly have been such a vicious killer. Lamphere vehemently denied any involvement. He also stated that Belle was alive and had fled the place before the fire.

Remains of One of the Victims

It turned out that there were a startling number of deaths in Belle's background. In 1900, her husband Mads Sorensen had died from "convulsions" after Belle had insured him for $8,500. Two of her adopted children (also insured) had died from conditions consistent with poisoning, and several of her insured establishments had burned down. Belle's second husband, Peter Gunness, hadn't lasted a year and she reported that a meat grinder and a jar of scalding water had somehow fallen on his head.

In short order, Belle had placed matrimonial ads in newspapers to lure men with money—many of whom had been at the farm for a brief stay before they disappeared, like Andrew Helgelein. Some had left their personal effects behind. In fact, Helgelein was identified as the first body pulled from the ground.

Neighbors recalled that Belle had recently brought in a derelict woman whose physical dimensions resembled the headless corpse, so a debate ensued over whether Belle had pulled a fast one, deciding to fake her death after Helgelein's brother warned her he was coming. Her nearly empty bank account supported this possibility, as a calculation of the funds she'd taken from her many "visitors" totaled over $50,000.

Back in Italy, Lombroso reviewed the case and offered his statement. He asserted that among deviant types, females were worse than males. "It is not enough for a woman to murder an enemy," he said, "she wants to make him suffer, and she enjoys his death." A true female degenerate like Belle Gunness would lack a maternal instinct, Lombroso added, and would find pleasure in torturing others, even her children. "Knowing [that] the feminine criminals always mix eroticism with crime," he said, "Mrs. Gunness must have used to obtain her accomplices besides the attraction of gain the attraction of sexuality."

A jury decided that Lamphere was guilty of arson, but that evidence of murder was lacking. Gunness was allegedly sighted numerous times around the country, and the best candidate was a woman named Esther Carlson, arrested in 1931, in Los Angeles, for fraud and murder. Before her trial commenced, she died, so nothing was ever proven.

Around 1930, another house was built on the burned-out foundation, and several excavations turned up bones, but they were not confirmed as human. Ghost hunters who have explored the grounds offer some intriguing findings. A group known as the

Indiana Ghost Trackers reports that over the past century there have been suicides on this property and that the ghost of Belle, herself, has shown up in several La Porte shops.

Given how many people were murdered here, one might expect much more activity, but stories are few.

Back to Lombroso's Ghosts

The Gunness analysis was the last sensational case to which Lombroso applied his theory. Just short of his sixty-fourth birthday in 1909, he died from angina. The year before, he had published a startling book, *After Death, What?* In the midst of his focus on science, Lombroso had developed a passionate interest in the paranormal.

"If ever there was an individual in the world opposed to spiritism by virtue of scientific education.... I was that person," he wrote. Having steadfastly believed that everything was reducible to physical matter, including the soul, in 1891 he set out to observe a séance.

After witnessing objects inexplicably moving on their own through the air, Lombroso resolved to look into teleportation. He learned about a talented medium, Eusapia Palladino, and with other professionals he attended seventeen of her gatherings.

Séance with Eusapia Palladino

22

They took precautions, such as searching her, changing her garments, holding her hands and feet, and taking charge of the light on the table. Even under these conditions, things happened.

She would write on a tablet, and while no writing appeared on the surface, it would be found deeper inside the tablet. Or she would make a hand appear that grasped things and touched people. It once made imprints in soft clay. She could also create death masks of known people who had died by placing clay wrapped in linen inside a box and calling on the person's spirit to appear.

During one séance, Lombroso was shocked by a short ghostly figure that resembled his deceased mother. It spoke to him, removed a veil, and kissed him. He reportedly saw this figure over a dozen times afterward and felt ashamed at having so firmly opposed the possibility of psychic phenomena. Against the recommendations of his colleagues, he published his book about spirit mediums, but because he died that year he suffered little professional backlash. Like a true scientist, he believed in an open mind.

Lombroso's writings on the subject are intriguing. He recounts the various types of paranormalists as typtological mediums who communicated by table tapping, motor mediums who caused furniture to move, painter mediums, speaking mediums, rhabdomancists who located metals in the earth, pneumatographers who could manifest writing without a writing implement, dematerializers who attracted objects to come through from some other place, and photfors who "bring out gleams of light." The list goes on, always with the same idea: people who could perform seemingly impossible feats with the assistance of spirits.

Lombroso relates this tale from Boccaccio, who penned *The Life of Dante*. It seems that after Dante Alighieri died, his sons found some of his unfinished works. They decided to complete the task, and one, Jacopo, had a vision of his father in white garments, surrounded by light. In the vision, Jacopo asked his father the location of the missing part of his work. The figure took him by the hand into his former sleeping chambers and touched a spot on the wall.

Jacopo woke up, sought out a friend of his father's to serve as a witness, and went into his father's former bedroom. They discovered a small window behind a blind, and when they opened it they discovered several moldy manuscripts. On these fragile pages,

Dante had penned thirteen cantos that completed the work with which his sons had been concerned.

Among the tales verified for a period of three years by a number of "the most eminent English experimenters" was the case of Katie King. Florence Cook took up the life of a psychic after viewing levitation at a séance, taking possession of the spirit form of a blond woman who called herself Katie King. (By other accounts, she was Annie Owen Morgan, daughter of a pirate. She had murdered her own children.) Supposedly, it was possible to photograph her and even measure her heartbeat (five beats per minute less than Florence's heart).

Lombroso's concluded that there was sufficient evidence from his observations and those of his colleagues to state that "there exists an immense series of psychical phenomena that completely elude the laws of psychophysiology." However, he thought that people who had the most access to them were subject to neurological states that de-activated the thinking brain, including hysteria, being in a trance, and dreaming.

Paranormal activity worked best, he thought, through "the actions of the unconscious." In fact, Lombroso hypothesized that the entities were relying on the brainpower of the living, so that their own intelligence would be fragmentary, even confused. One discarnate form said that communication was like a phone call from a long distance. (Keep in mind they did not have "smart" phones.) The "heavy atmosphere" buffered it.

Lombroso was prescient. Scientists have established that the brain operates within several different-frequencied "waves" and have identified and named them: theta, beta, delta and alpha. Percipients to the paranormal will often speak of being in a relaxed, day-dreamy-like state just before the event. This coincides with the alpha state in the brain. During sleep, it is the state just barely below consciousness in which dreams are formed. (And since paranormal events cannot be predicted, it is difficult to set up an experiment to test percipients' brain activity or body chemistry.)

Bearing the alpha state in mind, G. P.'s next communication is interesting.

"In order to speak with you," G. P. wrote via Piper, "It is necessary for me to re-enter the body and there dream. Hence, you must pardon my errors." Becoming disincarnate was a severe, disorienting shock. Communicating, he said, was like trying to climb up inside the trunk of a hollow tree. Mediums were "lighthouses," while those without such powers were hardly visible.

At times, Lombroso's acceptance of spirit manifestations seems remarkably naïve for a man of science, but science back then was limited to controlled situations, statistical analysis, and replicable experiences—especially for such elusive phenomenon. Still, Lombroso models the attitude to which we aspire: go look for yourself, dismiss nothing outright, and accept nothing outright.

With this inspiration, we'll move on.

Early Electronic Evidence

Katherine went to Savannah, Georgia, with a crew from Court TV to the former home of Conrad Aiken, an award-winning American novelist and poet. She tells this tale.

My first task was to learn more about him and the crime committed in his home. He'd lived in a beautiful 4,200 square foot row house at 228 East Oglethorpe Street, across from the Old Colonial Cemetery, in the oldest part of Savannah. Conrad knew by the age of nine he wanted to be a poet and he often scared himself by reading the poems and tales of Edgar Allan Poe.

His home life, as the elder brother of four, was under constant tension as his parents argued bitterly. Aiken's father, William Ford Aiken, was a mentally unstable genius who feared that his family would one day institutionalize him. In contrast to his paranoia, his wife, Anna, was a wannabe-socialite. Among their arguments was the typical domestic squabble over money. This is what they were fighting about on February 27, 1901, when Conrad was just 11 years old.

The boy heard his father count to three and then a scream from his mother, followed by a loud "pop." Then a second shot. The boy ran to see what had happened and found both of his parents dead on the floor of their bedroom.

Aiken's father had shot his wife and killed himself. Shocked, Conrad ran for the police.

Now orphaned, his siblings went to one relative, while he was sent to an aunt in Massachusetts. Eventually, Aiken went to Harvard, won the Pulitzer Prize, married three times, and became lifelong friends with poet T. S. Eliot. In 1950, he was named the Poet Laureate of the United States. For the last eleven years of his life, Aiken returned to Savannah, living next door to his childhood home.

Interested in Freudian psychology, he lived with a deep fear of inherited insanity. Throughout his work, Aiken explored the messages of his subconscious, believing that understanding his motivations was the key to self-awareness. The magic of Aiken's poetry, some critics have said, lies in its ability to suggest through sound and rhythm things that are beyond the easy reach of rational consciousness. This begins to sound like something in the paranormal.

Aiken spent a lot of time in Bonaventure Cemetery, where his parents were buried, and a marble bench became his own tombstone there. It was immortalized when characters in John Berendt's *Midnight in the Garden of Good and Evil* sat on it to drink mint juleps.

Aiken Row House in Savannah, Georgia

Our crew arrived by invitation at 228 East Oglethorpe with an infrared video camera and several digital voice recorders. I was with a reporter from Los Angeles named Tori. I set a voice recorder out on the porch and another in the room believed to have been Conrad's bedroom, near the master bedroom where the murder-suicide had occurred. Downstairs, the front door slammed shut. It could have been a breeze, of course, but it startled us.

In the master bedroom, Tori and I sat on the bare hardwood floor. This was new to Tori, so I spent some time explaining to her how to ask a question and wait a few moments before asking another. To one question that she asked me about the procedure, we received a distinct, "Yes!" on the recorder. Neither of us had said it. While we were discussing logistics (with the recorder running), we caught an emphatic whisper that said, "You want to know what I know."

We did, indeed, but as hard as we tried we could not induce whoever had whispered to say something more.

Later, in the basement, when we asked for a name, we recorded what sounded like a child whispering, "Ho." Fairly quickly after that, another voice—a different one—said, "Who's the girl?" One of the voice analysts who helped us put it all on tape said there was yet another voice that asked, "Who has the key?"

Although there was no indication that any of the voices were related to the deceased, or even to the poet who once had lived in this house and witnessed a tragedy, their presence suggests that certain emotionally charged incidents may not only help trap, but also attract paranormal forces. (Of course, we were also very close to a large cemetery.)

Mark and Katherine started exploring electronic voice phenomena (EVP) during the 1990s, when ghost-hunting groups had just begun experimenting with digital recorders. Together and apart, we set up experiments. We also looked into the history of EVP to find out more about the very earliest efforts, long before digital technology was even known. Since forensics involves such things as audio and voiceprint analysis, EVP joins these two realms. What follows is the background that informed and inspired us.

Documented Voices

Apparently as far back as the 1920s, inventors like Thomas Edison and Guglielmo Marconi had attempted to develop some kind of recording device for communicating with the dead. It wasn't until 1936, however, that Atilla von Szalay tried to record the voices that he had heard while in a dark room developing photos. He managed it in 1945 on a wire recorder, but the voices were too faint to prove anything. He resumed his recordings in 1956 with magnetic audiotape, and Raymond Bayless joined him. They published a paper in *The Journal of the American Society for Psychical Research*, but no one responded.

The person actually credited with the earliest recording of EVP was Friedrich Jürgenson, sometimes called the Father of EVP. He was a man of many talents and connections. A Scandinavian artist, archaeologist and opera singer, he knew nearly a dozen languages, a skill that turned out to be quite handy. The Vatican asked him to catalogue its archaeological wonders, as well as to paint the Pope's portrait, which he did several times. Jürgenson spent a great deal of time excavating the buried city of Pompeii.

At times, Jürgenson experienced moments in which whole sentences entered his consciousness. "It was all soundless," he said, but he recognized the words and phrases as a "deformed" form of English. During the spring of 1959, he received a message about an investigation station in space and deciphered it to mean that someone—or something—was conducting a series of observations of humans. Supposedly, magnetic radars were transmitted in batches of thousands, which humans were unable to see or sense. Jürgenson thought he might be able to capture some of this on tape. He tried but failed to record communications from outer space.

Jürgenson's stint with recording EVP occurred rather serendipitously. That June, he and his wife went to their country house, where he hoped to record some bird songs. He had a special fondness for a certain type of finch. One morning, he set up his machine. The birds were active and he expected to get some clear recordings. He pressed the record button, let it run for a while, and then rewound the tape. He hit the button that would let him hear the final product.

To his surprise, he heard a vibrating type of noise, which buffered the sound of the birds. They sounded as if they were at quite a distance. He thought that a tube inside the recorder might be damaged.

"Then I heard a trumpet solo," Jürgenson wrote, "a kind of signal for attention. Stunned, I continued to listen when suddenly a man's voice began to speak in Norwegian. Even though the voice was quite low, I could clearly hear and understand the words. The man spoke about 'nightly bird voices' and I perceived a row of piping, splashing, and rattling sounds."

But then the noises stopped. At that moment, he could hear the birds as if he'd recorded them the way he'd initially tried. "The machine worked perfectly." So, the machine was not damaged. For those few moments, something had displaced the birds.

Jürgenson tried to get more samples, wondering if this interruption had been some kind of alien communication. However, he'd *understood* the voice. What alien would be speaking in Norwegian? Since the voice had been disembodied, he pondered the possibility that it was from a person no longer alive. He thought the voice might have been from the Other Side.

He kept recording. Finally one day, he got a rather remarkable result. "When I listened to the tape," he stated, "a voice was heard to say, 'Friedel, can you hear me? It's Mammy.'"

He had to play this back several times, hardly believing what he was hearing.

"It was my dead mother's voice," he reported. "'Friedel' was her special nickname for me." It was clear to him that communication with the dead was possible.

Jürgenson immediately abandoned his painting career and focused on making recordings of the dead. His effort paid off. He received more messages, but they were fragmented. He did not achieve two-way communication, but he was encouraged. In 1964, he published a book. In it, he wrote, "I had never before been so touched and captured by any other urgencies than by these mystical connections, literally floating in the ether."

Several educational institutions took an interest in Jürgenson's work. He offered demonstrations of how he would set up a simple microphone, set his recorder to 'record,' and then speak into the room, allowing time for the voices to respond. When he played the tapes, he often had to play them at slower speeds in order to hear the voice impressions left there. Because he knew so many languages, he was able to identify voices that spoke Swedish, German, Russian, English, and Italian.

One voice urged him to use a radio as a medium, so he connected a microphone and a radio receiver together to the recorder. He found he could now converse with some of the voices. However, he had opened himself to the criticism that he was just receiving radio signals from various stations. He ignored these comments and published two more books on EVP. When he died 1987, he had made several hundred tapes of disembodied voices in a multitude of languages.

A man who'd visited Jürgenson to learn more about this phenomenon was a skeptical Latvian named Konstantin Raudive. In 1965, he set up his own experiments with recording the dead. Although nothing happened for three long months, he persevered. Then he got results. A *lot* of results. Raudive became so obsessed with EVP that he devoted twelve hours a day to his experiments. Within three years from when he began, he published his own book, *The Inaudible Made Audible*, claiming to have recorded over 72,000 EVP messages in many different languages. This book was translated into English as *Breakthrough*. He agreed to be tested in soundproof booths, and still he got impressive results. Raudive seemed to have become an EVP magnet.

There was also a book, *Phone Calls from the Dead*, by D. Scott Rogo, which documented numerous accounts in various places of people who had received calls from, and conversed with, dead people whom they knew. Sometimes they realized the person was dead; other times they only found out later. We'll discuss those phone calls (and Rogo) later.

Networks

Others were carrying on experiments independent of Raudive and getting similar results. William Welch was among them. He was interested in finding some mechanical means for communicating with those who had passed on, whom he dubbed "technicians." He envisioned them working as diligently as he was on ways to break through. At one point, he mentioned that they might be able to help "receivers" (us) improve our abilities.

George Meek, a research engineer, found a way to accelerate the development of paranormal connections. Author John Fuller met and wrote about him. According to Fuller's account, Meek told him that the ghost of a NASA scientist, Dr. George Mueller, had visited an uneducated man in Pennsylvania named Bill O'Neil, who possessed mediumistic abilities. Mueller had died fourteen years earlier, but he wanted to help O'Neil design some equipment that operated at 29 megahertz that would facilitate two-way communication between them.

O'Neil had contacted the editor of a paranormal magazine, who'd put him in touch with Meek. When Meek met O'Neil and checked out what Mueller had offered thus far (his social security number, his career history, and unlisted phone numbers of colleagues), he believed that what O'Neil said was possible. Meek then funded O'Neil's efforts to continue to get information, and he helped build a complicated device that would achieve their dreams.

It was called Spiricom. After months of futile experimentation, on October 27, 1977, the first voice came through. Instead of the typical brief and mundane comments often recorded for EVP, this was a real conversation. The content concerned getting the controls right.

They got nothing more for quite some time, but by 1980 they reportedly had held over twenty hours of extended dialogue. They gave out the plans to others, but no one else could replicate their results. John Fuller eventually wrote a book about Meek and his Spiricom called, *The Ghost of 29 Megacycles*.

This effort got the attention of people around the world who were experimenting with EVP. Many groups set about learning this technology and improving it. In 1982, Sarah Estep started the American Association—Electronic Voice Phenomena (AA-EVP), joining together hundreds of experimenters in many different countries. In 1976, using an old recorder, she decided to try it herself for a week. Each morning and each evening, she recorded for two hours, asking basic questions such as "Is anyone here?" But she received no responses.

Growing bored, she decided to change her question to "What is your world like?" To her surprise, she recorded a voice that said, "Beauty." She started recording daily, to continue to try to achieve contact. The messages were brief, such as "We're going to help you." She reported that receivers frequently get requests for help, prayers, and guidance from souls who seemed unaware they were dead. In *Voices of Eternity*, she reported her many results.

According to Estep, the spirits are drawn to researchers or brought to them by entities whose job it is to rescue lost souls. The messages sometimes appeared to be warnings of what it means to be unprepared for death. She felt certain that these entities were trying to help us to improve our lives and connect with them for some higher purpose.

Spiricom ushered in the new field known as ITC, or Instrumental Transcommunication—the use of multiple electronic systems for the purpose of communication. In 1983, Hans-Otto Koenig in West Germany developed equipment that used low-frequency oscillators. An acoustics expert, he was invited onto an international radio show to demonstrate ITC. Koenig carefully set up his equipment under the scrutiny of the station's engineers. When someone asked if they could get a direct response, a voice came through with, "Otto Koenig makes wireless with the dead." It was a stunning moment, and it wasn't long before audio-video contact was also established and spirit images were seen on televisions.

It seemed that electromagnetic energy was a crucial factor in successful communication. Some people believe that we all have a certain amount of energy and that groups of people get better results because they collectively make more energy available as a contact medium. Having fun and maintaining a playful attitude appeared to help researchers get the best results—again, high energy.

The studies of bioelectricity in virtually every part of the human body were confirmed in the 1980s by Dr. Robert O. Becker and resulted in his book *The Body Electric*. The work of Dr. Valerie V. Hunt demonstrated that the electrical field extends beyond the physical body in a field around it and is susceptible to changing frequencies according to various factors. She recorded her work in a book, *Infinite Mind*. The questions arise: Are these sources of energy made available to the denizens of the Other World for their use in communicating; Is this energy, as the Laws of Thermodynamics appear to state, indestructible and therefore immortal?

During the 1990s, an international organization was formed for cooperation among researchers of ITC, which flourished for two years. "Enhanced ITC" included telephone conversations with spirits, pictures of the dead on television, extended messages through the radio, images through the fax, and text on computers. Perhaps not so surprisingly, it seemed that some of that first generation of EVP researchers, such as Jürgenson and Raudive, had returned as spirits to the next generation to assist them with refining the methods. They gave specific instructions about equipment and offered brief descriptions of the Other Side. Scientists in several countries collected impressive technological data from several voices that collectively referred to themselves as TimeStream. They wanted to help, although they said that being a spirit was not like anything that any living person could imagine. It was wondrous, and quite busy.

From this history, we were able to compile a consensus about EVP.

- We can hear spirits talking among themselves as they wait to communicate;
- White noise or humming seems to facilitate the voices;
- An acoustic window seems to open randomly, and briefly.

EVP recording continues today with more sophisticated techniques, so the early attempts provided an important base. Controlled studies are essential to the credibility of this resource.

Our EVP

Recording electronic phenomena is done in context, so let's lay out some preliminary information for paranormal investigations. As we said before, there are four basic types of equipment: detecting, recording, communicating, and analytical. The typical "ghost investigation" today goes like this:

1. Preliminary Investigation: A small investigation team will take a medium, whom is kept clueless about the nature of the history or hauntings, to a site. They use recorders to interview the percipients of the ghostly events and may attempt to get EVP recordings from the deceased. They also record through notes, voice recordings, and still photos the medium's reactions. After the initial walk-through, they all meet and the medium reveals his or her findings.

2. Primary Investigation: A full team such as ours conducts a more thorough investigation during the day. (Contrary to what you see on television, it's not necessary to conduct a paranormal investigation during the night. That "ghosts only come out at night" is a ridiculous myth; they can be recorded or photographed any time of day or night. Since the safety of the team is paramount, a daylight investigation is nearly always attempted unless circumstances such as business hours or owner restrictions dictate otherwise.)Videographers and still photographers attempt to capture spirit images at specific sites identified by the owner of the haunted site or the medium, or where electromagnetic field meters (EMF) and quick-read thermometers react. Daylight photos of spirit energies are attempted indoors and out using the "Crownover Technique" of infrared filters and settings. With a recorder, one person may ask questions, such as, "What happened to you here?" "Were you injured?" "How old are you?" Some voices have identified themselves by name, offered the year they believe it is, or explained how they died. The medium's input may help to supply a starting point for communications. Techniques are constantly improving through experiment and technology. For

example, the advent of the digital camera, which captures images a little farther into the infrared or ultraviolet ends of the light spectrum; specially designed digital audio recorders have been developed to attempt to establish two-way communication with the dead; and experimental strobe infrared/ultraviolet lights to capture energy frequencies that vibrate in and out of visual range. If the area can be secured overnight, special infrared/motion detecting cameras can be placed in locked areas to detect and record movement. While technology is utilized, sometimes "old school" works as well: communication can often be established using dowsing rods and pendulums. Later that information can be tested against documented facts regarding the site.

3. Analysis: The team downloads photographs, videos and audio recordings into computers and uses specific programs to analyze the data. Audio computer software graphically portrays sound— interestingly enough, showing that the EVP "voices" are within the human range of sound. Analysis using earphones and repetition will usually reveal words and, sometimes, full sentences. The team then writes a report, downloads all recordings to disks, and files it. If the paranormal investigation is being conducted in conjunction with a criminal investigation, the data can be made available to the police or criminal investigators for leads or for questioning suspects. Imagine: A suspect is being questioned and the investigator hits him with a bit of information known only to the suspect and the deceased victim, "smoking out" the suspect.

Ghosts can make terrific witnesses…once we get them to talk! We'll tell you such tales as we move along. But first, some background on a collective effort to be scientifically rigorous about paranormal phenomena.

The Science of Ghosting

First Research Societies

Two related groups, one British and one American, made the first organized effort to approach paranormal phenomena in a measured, objective, and controlled manner. It was inspired during the 19th century by the emerging embrace of the scientific method crossing paths with a popular 1848 publication, *The Night Side of Nature*. Author Catherine Crowe used her collection of creepy tales not just to entertain but also to challenge scientists. They were too quick to dismiss paranormal narratives by stable citizens, she said, and she wanted "a few capable persons" to undertake a proper investigation.

During the 1850s, a team of Harvard professors attempted to respond by investigating a sideshow allegedly aided by spooks, but they resolved nothing. Years later, another Harvard professor, William James, observed that "the ideal of every science is that of a closed and completed system of truth." Thus, scientists who could not reconcile ghost tales with their systems simply discredited the narratives. James rightly thought this was intellectually dishonest. We still encounter this attitude, and since we're trying to blend science into our paranormal pursuits, we discussed it with Gregg McCrary.

"When you frame an issue," Gregg said, "you look only for evidence that fits within the frame and discount things that don't fit. But the frame has to be permeable. You have to let new things in."

"The fact that we're still dealing with closed mindsets over a century later," Katherine said, "just shows who we are as humans."

"It becomes confirmation bias," Gregg added. "It feels good to be affirmed in what you believe."

"Maybe we need to be satisfied in a certain way for information to be cogent for us," Mark said. "It's not so much a framework."

"From the investigative perspectives" Gregg responded, "if you have a dead body and you call it a suicide, you investigate it one way. If it's a homicide, you go another way. Once you frame it, all sorts of things follow. That's the danger of labeling."

"But you need *something*," Katherine said. "You need a guide in order to move forward.

"You need a narrative, but you have to be careful about the weight you put on early information. You tend to go with what you heard initially. I think the problem with this stuff is that people lock it out altogether. I'm a skeptic, but I'm willing to be shown that it works. It's our job to find facts."

"We've been prejudiced for so long," Mark added. "When we were kids, we had ideas of ghosts: they were scary, they showed up at night, it was some tortured human being. We get these ideas from TV. But now we find that virtually everything we once believed is wrong. For example, most of my stories occurred during the day."

"So we know what James and his gang were up against," Katherine stated, "because we're still dealing with it today. But it's antithetical to the investigative spirit, so to speak."

British Cousins Henry Sidgwick (a classics professor) and Edward White Benson (future archbishop of Canterbury) founded The Ghost Society at Cambridge. Together, they outed numerous fraudulent mediums, but Sidgwick believed there might be something genuine in paranormal phenomena. One of his students, Frederick Myers, joined him. In 1882, they became two of the three founding members of the Society for Psychical Research (SPR). This movement gained momentum throughout the latter half of the 19th century.

William James met with the SPR and participated in some of its investigations. In 1885, James became part of the effort to form a sister organization in the States, the American Society for Psychical Research (ASPR). He also founded the Lawrence Scientific School to subject paranormal claims to scientific study. For twenty years, until his death, he served as a visible leader in the movement.

William James

James discovered the Boston medium, Leonora Piper, who seemed to possess a genuine gift for attracting spirits. (She's the medium through whom George Pelham

37

communicated.) However, no matter how much effort he put into his search for proof of life after death (especially when several like-minded investigators died), he reached the end of his life disappointed.

Despite being impressed, at times, that he'd received a genuine communication from the spirit of a deceased friend, he thought the data problematic. The spirit could describe incidents with which James was familiar, but could call up nothing from its own childhood or personal life. James hypothesized that telepathy (the medium reading his mind) was a better explanation than an actual spirit. James wondered if there might be a metaphysical reason for keeping the Other Side a mystery. In his final essay on the subject, James wrote that it might be unfair to expect purity in such elusive experiences. Perhaps science could not answer all questions.

Supposedly, after James died, he communicated through several mediums, but no one managed to prove it. His wife had traveled from one medium to another to achieve some form of communication, but she received no message. A few former associates said that a spirit had reproduced conversations that they remembered, but in the end, no one could say for sure. But the efforts to prove the existence of spirits continued.

Philip

In 1972, the Toronto New Horizons Research Foundation decided to see if they could create ghostly effects like those reported by people at séances. They would use similar contexts and devices, e.g., a séance. They designed a ghost, which they named "Philip." They gave Philip a tragic history as an English aristocrat born in 1624. They listed his habits, customs, physical features, and associates. He'd even had an affair. When he was 30, he'd committed suicide.

The group's eight members knew Philip's entire history and they came together for regular meetings. They discussed Philip as if he'd been an actual person and tried to achieve contact. After doing this activity for several months, they heard raps or "answers" on the table in response to their questions, just like at a genuine séance. The table even moved on its own and once shot across the room. The group experienced cool breezes and saw metal bend. They caught all of this on video cameras. Devising a code, they got the spirit to answer questions about himself, but he could offer only information that the group had made up.

The researchers believed they had successfully proven that ghostly phenomena derive from psychological projection. When another group joined them and tried to get EVP, they were unsuccessful.

In 1974, a different group produced a similar set of manifestations. They named their "collective hallucination" Lillith. She, too, received a tragic history, and she made noises for them much quicker than Philip had for his group. One evening, the two groups converged to enjoy the attentions of their respective entities. A third group created "Sebastian."

We might assume from these efforts, then, that all ghostly phenomena might be merely psychological in nature. Electricity powers the human brain, so it wouldn't be surprising if the mind was the basis for phantom incidents. Some scientists accept this notion.

Brain Studies

When Dr. Rick Strassman performed a series of experiments with N,Ndimethyltryptamine or DMT, he interpreted the results in his subjects as the key to understanding the euphoria of mystical experiences. DMT is a plant-derived chemical also made in the human brain that was first discovered in 1931 when a Canadian chemist synthesized it from tryptamine (from which LSD and serotonin are derived). Then it was associated with the plants known to produce psychedelic effects, and in 1955, a researcher in Budapest injected some. He experienced tingling, elevation of blood pressure, visual hallucinations, and euphoria. Later researchers who followed his lead felt as if they were flying and one woman observed the presence of godlike beings.

Next, DMT was discovered in the human brain, making it the first endogenous human psychedelic. Eventually Strassman found that DMT was closely related to the neurotransmitter, serotonin, which is involved in mood, perception, and thought. The brain breaks down DMT for normal brain functions, but when the concentration gets too high, weird effects result.

From 1990 to 1995, Strassman conducted clinical research at the University of New Mexico's School of Medicine with sixty volunteers who agreed to go through trials of increasing DMT strength. He kept exact records of what these subjects said under the influence and noted how they often reported visions and experiences that sounded like people who'd described alien encounters, ghostly beings, and near-death experiences. He theorized that it might facilitate spiritual transitions via profoundly expanded consciousness.

The subjects drank DMT-laced tea and smoked DMT. They soon reported visions and a feeling that their consciousness was separating from their bodies. They also experienced the "presence" of entities. Then they were given a more powerful form of DMT through intravenous injections. Some heard inner voices, some were confused, some elated. While on the drug, they behaved in ways they could not recall later, but they did remember the feeling of losing boundaries.

One finding was that the context in which DMT was taken had a strong influence on the quality and type of experience. If the subject was hoping for a transcendent experience, then that's where their experience tended to go. If they were afraid, then anxiety was pronounced. Strassman surmised that DMT shifted the brain's ability to become a spiritual receptor.

In the discipline known as neurotheology, scientists studying specific regions of the brain have explored "the science of belief." Andrew Newberg, a professor of religious studies at the University of Pennsylvania, and assistant professor in radiology in their Division of Nuclear Medicine, believes there is a biological basis for spiritual hunger. Newberg teamed up with Eugene d'Aquili, an anthropologist who had proposed this idea back in the 1970s. Together they used brain-imaging technology to find out what goes on inside the head during mystical states.

Using subjects who engaged in an intense prayer session or immersed themselves in the peak moments of Buddhist meditation, the researchers applied a SPECT, or single photon emission computed tomography scan, which uses radioactive dye to take "photographs" of the way blood flows through the brain. The subject would go through his or her usual course of meditation, reach a deep state, signal it with a string, and then allow the dye to be injected through an intravenous tube. The SPECT camera then recorded the radioactive emissions via the tracer dye that circulated through the brain, carried by the flow of blood.

The tracer quickly locked into the brain cells and remained in place so as to get an accurate map of the brain as closely as possible to the moment of peak experience. The subject later described the feelings and experiences they had in order to compare them against the patterns shown by the dye.

Looking over the resulting images, the researchers noted something unusual about the orientation association area (OAA) in the left parietal lobe. The OAA's chief function is to help us get oriented in three-dimensional reality. Normal blood flow in the OAA indicates that the neurons are firing. The stronger the blood flow, the more activity. During states of deep meditation, the blood flow thinned out, depriving the OAA of information. This would give the subject the feeling of freedom from boundaries and limits. It's the ego's version of weightlessness, which some view as the experience of merging with a higher consciousness.

In 2006, an article in *Nature* described how Swiss neuroscientists had induced in an epilepsy patient the same effects that people describe when they enter haunted spaces. During the examination of this patient prior to surgery, the neuroscientists stimulated an area of her brain. She reported an impression of someone standing behind her, a silent young man posing in a way that perfectly mirrored her position. He seemed quite real and even felt as if he was embracing her. The doctors believed that with this discovery they had proven that the brain is the basis for the impression of ghosts.

In the UK, other researchers took groups of people to reputedly haunted spots. They asked the subjects to describe their experiences and prior knowledge about the place and concluded that the experience of ghosts was the result of environmental cues. Although the spots inspired creepy feelings even in people who had no prior knowledge about the ghost stories associated with them, the researchers believed this was due to culturally formed perceptions; the subjects were responding to a stereotypically creepy appearance. The researchers added that mediums whom correctly identify a haunted place are merely sensitive to such visual cues.

Group Cohesion

Quite interesting is the work with infrasound, i.e., sound at a frequency too low to be detected by the human ear (about 16 or 17 hertz). Infrasonic waves have been studied since the 1960s, when a French scientist focused on impressions that hurt his ears and shook his lab, but could not be distinguished as noise. Infrasound can cause sensations of fear and awe, which might explain the vague uneasiness that people feel when they think some unseen presence is nearby.

In a 2003 experiment, infrasonic elements were introduced into a concert and the concert-goers were asked to rate various pieces of music. Those pieces that included infrasonic aspects invariably induced descriptions of anxiety, uneasiness, sorrow, chills, revulsion, and even fear. If infrasonic waves are present in certain areas, those areas might gain a reputation for being haunted.

Paranormalists have also tried to produce controlled studies. Among the most noted took place in Scole, Norfolk, in Britain. Three experienced psychical researchers from today's SPR came together for a period of two years to investigate the activities of the Scole group—three middle-aged couples—who claimed to be meeting with spirit guides that had produced a range of phenomena.

Among the activities were tape recordings of voices, spontaneous images in undeveloped film, objects appearing out of thin air (apports) under a bell jar placed on a table as suggested by the spirit "team", shadowy figures, moving furniture, and even sophisticated messages from renowned but deceased scientists. (One piece of evidence—a sketch that appeared on an unopened can of film when it was developed—was signed "TAE". When they compared the handwriting with an example from when he was living, they realized the signature belonged to Thomas Alva Edison who was helping them from the other side.) They produced communications from these spirits in several languages, and the investigators looked for evidence of deception or fraud. They were unable to identify any, so the Scole Report was published in 1999. It inspired a great deal of controversy.

In essence, the investigators pondered the question of just what counts as acceptable evidence of the paranormal. In the Scole group, one couple served as mediums through which the "guides" communicated. They sat in the dark in the "Scole Hole," wearing luminous wristbands so they could see one another's movements. Over the four-year period in which the mediums met, many spirit guides came and went. Points of light darted about the room, responding to spoken requests. Via the mediums, these spirits offered information and could be questioned and cross-examined, so it was clear to the scientists that information had not been prepared beforehand. They also witnessed what they believed was disembodied intelligence.

The investigators were rightly criticized for failing to use adequate safeguards against deception, but they argued in return that no amount of deception could account for the wide variety of phenomena they had witnessed—especially when they were interacting with spirits on highly technical subjects.

One apport had been an edition of the April 1, 1944, edition of the *Daily Mail*. A chemical analysis of the paper authenticated it as World War II-era newsprint. Its condition was too pristine even for a collector who had preserved it for 50 years. It carried an article about a woman who, allegedly now a ghost, had grown interested in the Scole Group's efforts.

Even today, the debate continues and the verdict is still out as to what this group ultimately proved.

The Nesbitt Team

Perhaps William James was correct that, in the strictest sense, the scientific method couldn't answer all questions. Perhaps there's another way to test paranormal "evidence" in context, without needing to provide conclusions to the larger philosophical questions.

So, back to forensics.

How might a paranormal team contribute to an investigation? Let's use an actual case to demonstrate.

In 2006, Steven B. Williams, a Denver-based Dee Jay, was missing. A friend of his, photographer Robert Knight, had not heard from him in a month. They tended to be in contact, even though they had gone their separate ways.

So let's say Knight calls an investigator like Gregg McCrary. It's a missing person case, so there's a protocol.

"There are two general possibilities," Gregg stated. "He has gone away intentionally, or something has happened. If he's gone on his own power, there would be some indication of planning and he left with money, clothing, a wallet, credit cards, things like that. For the other possibility, his clothes are still there, his bankcards are there and there's no unusual activity in his accounts.

"So, now we consider an accident, a suicide or a homicide. Initially you try to go down one of those roads. If there's no evidence he left, you have to ask about his state of mind. Was he despondent? Would he harm himself? This is basic victimology. There should be a set of preconditions for suicide, such as financial trouble or serious personal problems. If you think it's a possible suicide, then where would he go to do it? People tend to go to places that are familiar, meaningful, or comforting, so you'd look there."

"If it's a possible accident," Katherine added, "you'd have to ask if he likes to go hiking or if he drove his car somewhere—is his car missing? So, you'd eliminate that possibility with what you know about him."

"With a homicide," Gregg said, "people he knows would be the first suspects. Does he have enemies? Is someone angry at him? You find out what elevated his chance of becoming a victim of a homicide."

Victimology is a complex topic, but that's the idea. If we eliminate those scenarios, and he's not just dead from natural causes in his residence, and we're at a dead end for clues, we would call in paranormal resources.

In this case, Knight called on an associate involved in remote viewing. Many books have been written by those who took part in a government program to learn if remote viewing might be a viable (and cheap) way to spy on our enemies. The Stargate Program ran for two decades and offered provocative results. Essentially, in remote viewing, people look at random letters and numbers (such as map coordinates or addresses) before letting their minds relax and form images of distant people and places.

In the case of the missing Williams, Knight turned to Angela Thompson Smith for assistance. She had worked with a Princeton-based group, Princeton Engineering Anomalies Research team (P.E.A.R.S.) and had later taught remote viewing. In 2002, she'd founded the Nevada Remote Viewing Group. To work on the Williams case, she gathered an impressive team of experienced viewers: a retired airline captain, a civil engineer, a former Air Force nurse, a civilian Air Force contractor, a librarian, and a photographer.

Each was given a coordinate on which to focus. Each member undertook one to three hour-long sessions. They had an initial viewing of a photo of the missing man, but received no other information. Collectively, they got images of a body in water near Catalina Island off the coast of California. They thought it was caught in some netting.

On the same day that this group gave Knight its report, a body was found off Catalina Island. Knight heard about it and called the morgue. He offered several unique identifiers of his missing friend, which matched the John Doe, and Williams officially became a murder victim. The remote viewing session had assisted with a quick identification. He had been in the ocean for about two weeks.

The group also did a viewing of the suspect. Knight was aware of an investment advisor named Harvey Morrow, who had befriended Williams. He'd invested money for Williams, but then had disappeared. So had the money. So, the remote viewers went to work again. One of them sketched a boat with Morrow on board, and they thought it was somewhere in the British Virgin Islands.

Morrow was in fact in the Caribbean. When he went to Montana for a job, his boss learned that he was wanted in connection with a homicide. He was arrested and later convicted.

This use of a paranormal tool is a good demonstration of the convergence of efforts for a paranormal forensics team.

"If I felt confident in the group," Gregg said, after reading about the case, "I would use them again. There's credibility: it worked. Why not wander off the reservation when standard techniques come up empty. I'd go with what I know first, because the answers are more likely to come out with the standard stuff, but I'd use other tools like this if they showed promise for getting the facts."

It is interesting to note that one of the most talented remote viewers associated with the Stanford (University) Research Institute (one of several recognized institutes sponsoring psychic studies in the country) was a retired police commissioner from Burbank, California, named Patrick H. Price. Price readily admitted that he used his abilities to run down suspects. At first he attributed it to luck and intuition. Later, however, he got such a clear image of a crime that he could not have known about beforehand that he could not deny his psychic powers. He was so good at remote viewing, that he could read printed words at a specified site…miles away!

And this is just one paranormal tool. A paranormal team called into a forensic investigation would rely on more than just remote viewing.

Let's say that there's been a homicide in an apartment, but the investigation has gone cold. The team enters the site. Although it has been rented out again, their medium (who knows nothing about the place) senses unsettling energy. The current tenants may or may not pay attention to the small unexplainable things happening in the apartment—personal items disappearing and reappearing, footsteps heard in an empty room, a muttering white noise heard periodically with no source—but the team's medium grasps it instantly. Walking around, she steps toward one room and is struck by the mass of energy there. It is difficult for her to enter this room because she "feels" the emotions of the dead (rather than a clairvoyant who would see them, or a clairaudient who would hear them). She asks the team to set up equipment in this room.

Mark Nesbitt & Brad Christman Prepare for an Investigation

It is daylight, so one investigator begins photographing using the Crownover Technique—taking a series of infrared-filtered, panoramic photos of the room from a tripod-mounted camera. Later, he will set up an ultraviolet strobe as a detecting device and take photos. Another investigator sets up a computer and brings up a dictation program. She will attempt to gather EVP through the microphone. Possibly, the words will be displayed in script upon the computer screen, a modern form of "automatic writing." Yet another investigator works with the medium using a digital recorder. The medium says she is hearing the name of a woman: Sara.

The other investigator requests silence, turns on the recorder, which is set on "voice activation mode" and asks, "Sara, are you here with us?" He pauses nearly a minute in total silence, yet the recording indicator on the machine shows something being recorded. Two or three other questions are asked, ending with, "How did you die?" and "Who did this?" Again, in total silence, the recorder indicates something is being impressed upon it.

When it is played back, there are sounds, possibly words, seemingly answers. The investigators think they know what is being said, but so as not to influence each other's independent analysis, they make no indication. The EVP data will be downloaded to a computer for a voice analysis. The team members will independently analyze the sound later.

Because of some strange images that appeared during the infrared still photography session, it is determined that overnight photos should be taken. A video camera with "nite-shot" near infrared capabilities is set up on a tripod in a corner of the room. This will record for the first hour or so after the team leaves. They know that often a great deal of activity occurs just after a team exits and they would like to capture it.

The computer with the dictating software is left running, as is another digital recorder set on "voice activation." They also set up two hunter's infrared "gamecams." Originally developed to take infrared-triggered photos of animals, it has captured unexplainable images as well. One is set on "photo," the other on "video." They leave the area and lock up for the night.

The next morning they retrieve their equipment. The digital sound recorder indicates that 22 minutes of something have been recorded in what should have been a totally silent room. It is secured for later analysis. The tape on the video camera is rewound and it is noticed that there are numerous "orbs" floating in front of the lens. It's possibly dust or pollen, but, more intriguing is the fact that the camera went in and out of focus several times—something an automatically focusing camera does only when something moves in front of it to break the infrared focusing beam. Yet nothing appears in the frames. It is also secured for later analysis.

The "gamecams," have been triggered. Their digital chips need to be downloaded to a computer for analysis. (When analyzed they show misty areas and a full figured apparition of what seems to be a woman.) Finally, the computer screen is activated. There, on the screen, are four typed words: "I dead eight May" entered on the screen via the microphone and dictation software.

Later independent analysis of the EVP through the computer software brings the team to the conclusion that during the questioning in the room, several words were spoken. In answer to the question, "Sara, are you here with us?" there is a hissing, "Yesssss." To the question, "How did you die?" the investigators think they hear two syllables and the word "murmur." Analysis of the graphics on the computer indicates there might be a "d" in the word: It could be "murder." And finally, to the question, "Who did this?" there is a one syllable word. All agree that there is a hard "G" sound at the beginning, and possibly an "L" at the end. They conclude the word may be the name, "Gil."

Sara's estranged boyfriend at the time was Gil, who had moved to the area just a few weeks before Sara's death. With authorities present, they ask him a few probing questions, and he handles this easily until the investigator mentions the word "May" and "eight." It is the name of his sister who died at age eight. No one in his adopted town knew of her except himself… and Sara. The EVP is played for him and he loses his composure: He seems to recognize Sara's voice saying his name. From there, he begins to unravel and finally he reveals evidence that strongly suggests that he's Sara's killer.

This information would be delivered to police investigators, who should be encouraged by the lead. They might then be able to develop evidence, focusing on details in ways they might not otherwise have done. Although this scenario is just a hypothetical, for the purpose of demonstration of the range of tools available, such investigations have occurred with one or more tools (such as in the Williams case above), and we cover them in the pages that follow.

Emerging Technologies

On March 14, 2012, AOL posted a video about a guy named Tim in Dunmore, Pennsylvania, who claimed to have received emails from a dead person. It seems that in June 2011, Jack Froese died from heart failure. His closest friends, Tim among them, sorely missed him. They had been friends for seventeen years.

A few months later, Tim received an email, signed by Jack Froese, which referred to a conversation they'd had before Jack died. Tim was certain that no one but Jack could have known the details.

Jack's cousin, Jimmy, said he, too, had received an email, which he showed on camera. Jimmy had broken his leg, and Jack said he'd tried to warn him before it happened. The implied message was that spirits could watch over us, foresee the future, and possibly change the course of events. Bones thinks, "I wonder why he didn't just warn Jimmy in one of these emails?"

Both young men tried to return the emails to elicit a response, but neither received anything further.

So, are spirits now using the Internet to communicate? We've heard of them dialing people on a phone, showing up in TVs, and even using faxes. Why not an email?

Deception Detection

Many of us in the paranormal field are aware of people running scams that exploit the popularity of ghost activities and the hope that ghosts exist. They want to get a video to go viral on the Internet, for example, or perhaps get a book deal for their demon-infested house. Maybe they just seek some attention. Tim claimed that he had "checked a little bit" and realized that the emails were coming from Jack's personal account. However, Tim did not elaborate on what he'd done to check this out or why he was certain that Jack's account was "unhackable." He merely stated that no one else knew Jack's password.

We sent a link to this video to ask a forensic digital examiner to comment, but before we get to that, we noted that there's a psychological angle on this story as well. Katherine knows a few things about how to "read" people, so she looked more closely at this AOL/BBC video. She turned off the sound so she could better watch expressions and gestures. She also watched certain parts in slow motion.

Although Tim and Jimmy came across as genuinely surprised by the emails, Katherine thought there was good reason to believe that Tim's mother had found a way to get into Jack's account to send them.

First, her lack of emotionality when a reporter interviewed her made Katherine suspicious. This mother showed no surprise, no happiness that her departed son was "with them," and, above all, no disappointment that he hadn't sent an email to her. Second, she'd attested to the fact that she and Jack had enjoyed "something special," and yet, where was his message to her? She had urged Jack's friends to "just accept it as a gift" and she was glad that it helped them with their grieving.

Katherine watched this video of her several times at different speeds, with and without the audio, and she spotted behavioral signals that suggested benign deception.

But first, a brief lesson for people who interview tellers of ghost tales.

Kinesics is the scientific interpretation of body language. Anthropologist Ray Birdwhistle coined the term in 1952, based on the idea that spoken words convey information on two levels. One is verbal, the other nonverbal, and the latter includes voice tone, pauses, gestures, posture, inflections, facial expressions, and noise from the vocal cords.

Birdwhistle believed that all bodily movements have meaning, and he referred to nonverbal communication as "paralanguage." Within this frame, a "kineme" is a grammatical unit in which certain movements can be used interchangeably without changing the meaning. Birdwhistle found that the face and body carry over 70 percent of the burden of communication. Specialized kinesics also includes written statements.

Kinesic analysis is hard work. It requires determining from a variety of cues a subject's frame of mind. This allows observers to note such things as stress, personality disorders, attitudes, ego defenses, and incentives. The kinesics expert must accumulate a solid mental database of diverse, human-centered information before becoming proficient at reading people.

Deception detection is at the heart of kinesic research today. In general, people are poor lie detectors, because they tend to judge credibility on the basis of unreliable verbal and facial cues, they're uneducated about actual deceptive cues, and their prejudices thwart an accurate intuitive assessment. In addition, spoken words distract us from making keen observations. Proficient people readers, however, know a lot about the finer points of gestures and expressions.

The muscles around the mouth and eyes take part in facial expressions in explicit and identifiable ways. For example, a specific muscle in the forehead participates in fear, and its absence would indicate possible faking. Joy involves specific eye muscles. In our culture, touching, scratching, or leaning on a specific area of the face tends to have a distinct meaning: the center of the forehead indicates frustration, while the cheekbone is often about focus and concentration; touching lips suggests uncertainty, and touching the chin indicates calculation. The abrupt onset or departure of any emotion is an indicator of fakery.

More demanding of people readers are the subtlest clues from fleeting expressions. Our brains are wired to respond to certain universal expressions, including those that appear and disappear in a fraction of a second. Everyone can make certain expressions voluntarily, but the face also has an involuntary system. When a person is feeling something that contradicts the emotion he wishes to present, the unconscious system can still leak through. Expressions that appear fleetingly in the midst of a dominant expression, usually contradicting it, are micro-expressions.

Dr. Paul Ekman from the University of California, San Francisco, is the world's foremost expert on micro-expressions. His work is the basis for the television series, *Lie to Me*. The muscle movements (expansions and contractions) in basic expressions became the basis for his Facial Action Coding System (FACS).

Each expression, whether a smile or frown, goes through a series of stages. It has a moment of gathering, a peak, and a breaking point. True expressions have a natural flow onto and off of the face. A limited number are regularly useful. Ekman identified twenty-three combinations that were related to seven universal emotions: disgust, anger, sadness, joy, fear, contempt, and surprise. Micro-expressions play off these seven.

Few people are even aware of noticing a micro-expression, although their brain picks up the information. If we see a happy expression, and no micro-expression preceded it, we sense the person is happy. However, if a negative micro-expression preceded the smile, we would sense the expression as sinister or manipulative. The inconsistency gives us an uneasy feeling, no matter how broadly or how long the person smiles.

Despite the many formulas one can find in lie detection books, there is no single sign of deceit in itself, no telltale Pinocchio's nose. To predict the behaviors that distinguish a deceptive person, the people reader must learn a lot about that individual's emotional base (or default behaviors). Lies are best identified in context, when compared over a period of time to other deceptive behaviors or narratives.

Critical kinesic principles for investigators include establishing a subject's behavioral "constants," which become default or reference points. Then they look for deviations. Those deviating behaviors that appear in clusters are more likely to signal deception. (Another important principle is for interviewers to self-monitor to ensure that they are not contaminating the subject's response with unconscious encouragement or skepticism.)

One model of deception detection focuses on five categories of deceptive behavioral signals: liars tend to be less forthcoming, less positive, more tense, less compelling with their narratives, and yet offer narratives that are more polished and without imperfection. Researchers have found that lying can produce such physiological signals as a heightened pulse rate, dilated pupils, twitches, and certain facial expressions—especially when the stakes are high. However, truthful but anxious people might also display such symptoms, while some types of liars might not.

Behaviors of discomfort should alert investigators to be alert for deceptive clusters. This can include speech hesitations and pauses, a lack of spontaneity, taking longer to respond to questions, appearing to plan what they will say, and responses that seem too long or are irrelevant. In terms of kinesics, there might be increased shrugging, blinking, and nervous habits like stroking an arm or leg. Increased leg and foot movements might arise in response to specific themes during questioning, as might venting the body, such as when a person pulls a shirt or collar away. They might flush, hold their breath, blanch, keep their head unusually still, or reduce their typical hand gestures. Feet pointed toward an exit can be a telling signal of the desire to escape. These behaviors occur more often in those with motivation to deceive—possibly because they are trying to plan and control what they say.

Cognitive load is a key concept in lie detection, in that the intention to lie can add more effort to a presentation. Some researchers have found that liars take slightly longer to start answering questions, or show a rehearsed quality, as if they've already thought about what they might say when questioned. Yet they must be thinking all the time about what they're saying in order to keep their story straight. However, if they've planned well, they might actually jump in more quickly than truth-tellers, because they have their act in a nice package. They'll also repeat phrases and avoid self-incriminating information.

Back to Jack's mother: So, we don't have enough information to see her default behaviors, but we can still pay attention to certain things she did. Apart from the lack of emotion that we expect from a grieving mother, in two places on this tape, while she's being questioned she draws her mouth into a very tight gesture, as if to prevent herself from leaking a secret. Her eyebrows are not raised in a sincere openness but rather seem frozen in place. She also looks away from the reporter during crucial questions in a manner that indicates discomfort, and she seems to hold her head in a posture that is slightly defiant.

"Overall," said Katherine [as Bones], "my first fleeting impression and my final analytical impression is that Jack's mother had sent (or knew how to have someone else send) the emails as a gesture of comfort. She hoped that Jack's friends would just receive it in the 'spirit' in which it was intended. I didn't believe that she believed that her son had sent emails from the Other Side. It's possible that her gestures and expressions indicate discomfort, but no one forced her to appear on the tape. In my opinion, this tale lacks credibility."

Digital Examination

So, let's see what our digital examiner has to say. Of course, he did not have access to the cell phones that received the messages or to Jack's computer, but as director of the digital crimes lab in Lehigh County, Pennsylvania, Detective Joe Pochron has plenty of experience with how such a claim might be analyzed. As sweet as this story is, an investigator cannot just accept it at face value. Anyone's account is hackable, and who knows what Jack left behind that could have revealed his password?

Digital forensics (also known as cyber-forensics, computer forensics, or forensic informatics) is the application of legal concerns and activities to the digital technology arena, for the purpose of developing evidence or assisting an investigation. In this field, investigators must have specialized knowledge about all kinds of digital gadgets and the Internet, and they must keep up on cyber-innovations. Digital forensics has many subspecialties, any of which can involve gathering, storing, classifying, manipulating, and retrieving information.

Investigators may develop crime scene simulation/animation, enhance images or filter noises, recover digital evidence, track identity theft, decoy and ambush cyber-offenders, and prove computer fraud. Evidence can come from computer hard drives, cell phones, black boxes, RFID tags, digital cameras, memory devices, and any other digital instrument, and the investigator must apply techniques for searching databases quickly and effectively, without distorting the information.

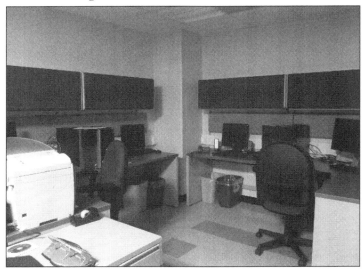

Digital Lab

Digital forensic specialists learn how to access a cell phone or computer to track whatever the user has done on it. They can recover deleted data, decode encrypted files, and restore corrupted files, as well as determine which websites a person has visited to acquire information or make contacts.

"First things first," Potion said. "Each email contains a header that will literally track the email from its originating I. P. address, which will provide a better understanding of where these emails came from. I'm not sure if Heaven has an Internet Service Provider (ISP), but if it does, this would show in the email header. The full email header is hidden from the user but is easily located; it just varies based on the email program or client. Once the header is checked and the originating I. P. address is located, I would contact the ISP and determine to whom the I. P. address is assigned on that date/time. If the case permits it or it is warranted, I would then go to the residence/business for possible examination of local machines to determine from which one the email was sent. I would also contact the email provider to get a list of user logs pertaining to logins and where they have originated."

If Jack's computer was used, and the mail came from his I. P. address, we'd want to check the times the emails were sent against what his mother was doing at those times. We would also press her more on her feelings about being left out of Jack's email recipient queue. At this time, her status remains suspicious, and we cannot accept that Jack's ghost definitely sent emails to his friends. Bones wants to know why the messages were so mundane.

What Is A Ghost?

We've discussed some history regarding ghostly appearances and communications. Let's get right to the theory with which we're operating. There are many theories about ghosts, from being souls of the dead to being mere psychological projections. A common definition that Mark uses when speaking to groups is that a ghost is a disembodied soul, which, after the life of the body is over, goes on to live an existence apart from the visible world. This definition encompasses several controversies: That there is more to human existence than the physical body—there is also a spirit or soul; that there is continued existence of this entity after the physical body dies; and that there is a place to which it goes that coexists with the visible world, but itself is invisible. The famous ghost hunter Hans Holzer's definition is more sinister: "Ghosts are the surviving mental faculties of people who died traumatically." In other words, to live on as a ghost by Holzer's definition, it's going to hurt!

Of course there are many debated theories concerning the subject.

The electrical impulse theory involves the notion that people who die suddenly, such as from suicide, murder, or an accident, become ghosts, because they emit a large electrical impulse into the physical environment. During periods of stress, such as battle or imminent death, the electrical impulses grow stronger. It is possible that they might produce energy that imprints itself on the atmosphere of a certain place, remaining there, though the person is now gone.

Polish physicist Janusz Slawinski, while studying the cause of the image on the famed Shroud of Turin, discovered that humans, upon death, give off a burst of photons 1,000 times greater than during normal everyday existence. He called it a "light shout." As well, human bones, because of their porosity, are piezoelectric and when broken also emit energy at that moment. It is theorized that the surrounding environment may somehow capture these bursts of energy, then released them under certain as yet unknown conditions. These sudden bursts of energy, when death is commonplace and bones are broken with great frequency, might explain why battlefields are considered some of the most haunted places on earth. In addition, many battlefields have an abundance of quartz-bearing granite rock which may act like the silicon chip in your computer to capture and store the bursts of electrical energy as the men are wounded and slain. Once we discover what the conditions are that release the information stored in the quartz, will we be able to then summon the ghostly energies at will?

Others speak of "time slips," where they find themselves in a completely different place, seeing people there as ghosts. They often see quite a few, or see buildings and vehicles no longer there—or even in existence. We've heard of entire battlefields populated with ghost soldiers, but since they didn't all die there, this can't be the kind of ghost we're after.

Then there's the issue of poltergeists, or "noisy ghosts" which arose in some places we investigated. The notion is that some mischievous spirit moves things around, throws items across rooms, hits or pinches people, and otherwise persistently makes life difficult. Many paranormalists believe that this is an energy manifestation from living people, typically adolescent or preadolescent children, but this notion doesn't really explain all such incidents. The question remains: Does the energy to move objects come from the adolescents or do the ghosts borrow the over-abundant energy from the children to do their mischief?

One more spooky manifestation is the "shadow person," which reveals itself as a dark form. In general, they are considered not quite human because their features, if seen, are distorted. Usually, as the legend goes, they flit out of view so fast it's difficult to know if anything was really there. They can supposedly disintegrate, move through walls, or just shoot away when there's danger that they might be fully seen. Some people have reported black shadows that were ominous and even hurtful. The sensation is often that they're just running through. If they raise any feelings, it's usually a chill or sense of dread—and always the impression of a full-bodied presence. Theories hold that they are the manifestation of a mass of negative energies, often deriving from some traumatic event, or that they are the residual energy of evil people.

Another theory relies on concepts from physics and psychology. Consciousness, reason, and emotion are components of the mind. When a person is physically alive, the mind and body form an inter-related unit, each part operating via a specific type of information-based energy. When consciousness leaves the body, it retains a residual body-awareness based in this energy, which resembles a memory. Body awareness fades unless certain patterns of emotional encoding from the mind/body connection anchor it to the body or some other form of information-based energy. Consciousness then becomes like a phantom limb, i.e. echoes of a former personality or ghostly phenomena, and the body memory becomes part of a memory field (which some physicists believe can exist independent of a brain).

"From my experience," Mark commented, "the electrical impulse theory has been proven because of the work of Slawinski."

"If you go back to the Tibetans," Gregg said, who had made a three-week trip to Tibet, "they describe a rainbow at the time of death of spiritual practitioners."

"There are also what some paranormalists call 'warps,'" Mark added, "or a 'tear in the fabric of time,' where we remain in our time period but get a glimpse of something from the past. This may be tied in with 'time slips'.

"As an investigator, it's not my job to believe or disbelieve. If people have had a similar experience independent of one another, this would imply that the haunting is real. But there's a possibility of contamination. They could have heard the story, even forgot that they had heard it. The stories are so similar, we have to consider it. People do internalize stories without realizing it."

"I agree," Katherine added. "Especially stories that have been published. People pick up things without knowing it and then think it happened to them. That's an issue with human memory that we find in the research over and over."

"I have several checks when I'm interviewing percipients of a ghostly event," Mark said. "Obviously, I won't reveal them all here, but, for example, one is if the story never changes from one telling to the next. When a person has a totally unique event in their life, like something paranormal happening, it is like the brain has taken a photo, and each time they recall it, it comes out almost exactly the same. Another check is for non-sequiturs. People will be telling their ghost story and all of a sudden they'll mention that a bird flew past, then continue with the story. The bird has nothing to do with the ghost story, but they're trying to tell the story exactly as it happened, so the bird is included."

We don't claim to know all the answers to paranormal phenomena, but that's why we keep investigating. In the next section we'll delve into specific aspects of forensic investigation that can dovetail with paranormal efforts, and how paranormal skills and methods can enhance forensic investigations. We'll start with the basics: a death investigation.

Death Investigation & Haunted Crime Scenes

On Monday, June 10, 1912, Mary Peckham noticed that her neighbor's home in Villisca, Iowa, was deathly quiet. She'd just seen J. B. Moore's family of six the evening before and she expected activity around the house by now. They had animals to feed. But the window curtains were drawn and it seemed that no chores were being done. Puzzled, Mary stepped on the porch and went to the door. She knocked and tried the knob. It was locked. She knew this was uncharacteristic. The Moores didn't lock their door. She went home to call Ross Moore, J. B.'s brother.

Mary's description disturbed him, so he came to the house. For the sake of protocol, he knocked. There was no answer. Ross tried looking through the windows, but they were covered, so he used his key to enter.

The place was silent, far too silent for a home with four young children. Ross cleared his throat and called out to J. B. No answer. He crossed the dark parlor toward the only bedroom on that floor. He opened it and stood still. He couldn't comprehend what he was seeing. Then he ran across the kitchen to exit the house. He needed the sheriff.

Hank Horton arrived, entered, and went straight to the door that Ross Moore had opened. Noting the dark interior and drawn curtains, he saw dark stains spattering the walls and two still forms beneath bed sheets. He knew what death smelled like: this. In the June heat in a closed house, it was rancid. He struck a match and saw that the white sheets were stained dark. Against the wall rested a long-handled ax with brownish stains on the blade.

Horton lit another match to find his way up the dark, steep staircase. Each step groaned from his weight, sounding hollow in the ominous silence. The smell of blood reached him again from the second floor, so he knew what he was in for.

At the top of the steps was a bedroom. Horton entered and saw even more sheet-covered forms and gore-splashed walls. Opening a curtain to let in some light, he knew exactly who he was looking at: J. B. and Sarah Moore. Both had received smashing blows to their skulls.

In the next bedroom, which held three beds, the spectacle was enough to bring a grown man to his knees. Horton raised the shade and saw that there were four dead children in this room, two of them lying in one bed. Blood drenched the bedclothes and spattered the walls and ceiling.

On that hot June morning in 1912, eight people had been slaughtered in the Moore home overnight, including two neighbor children who were visiting. An intruder had killed them all, one by one, with an ax.

Now the hard work began of looking for clues to who had done such a shocking act of violence against a respectable family so well-liked. A local physician and coroner joined the sheriff.

In the downstairs bedroom, the sheets were carefully lifted from the victims. Oddly, an item of clothing had been placed over the face of one—a gray coat like a boy would wear. The skulls and faces of each child were so smashed that no one recognized who they were. The younger girl, approximately 7, lay nearest the wall, and seemed relatively undisturbed. The physicians agreed that she'd likely died from the first blow, and the rest had been delivered postmortem.

The other child appeared to have been molested, or sexually posed. Her nightgown was up and she wore no underwear. One arm was over her head, under the pillow, and one leg was splayed outward. She appeared to have been turned over slightly to the right after she'd been bludgeoned. Her right knee bore a bloodstain as well, though there were no wounds to her legs or lower torso.

The person who had suffered the most was J. B. He'd apparently been struck repeatedly, in a form of overkill that indicated either rage or fear that the only adult male in the house could not be easily dispatched. His face had been chopped so often the eyes were gone.

Strangely, the coroner found a piece of a keychain and a four-pound slab of raw bacon wrapped in a cloth and lying on the floor in the downstairs bedroom, near the ax. Another piece, nearly the same size, was in the icebox in the kitchen. On a table stood a bowl containing bloody water and a plate of food, prepared but not consumed. The only other potential pieces of physical evidence were ripped items of clothing that covered a glass and several mirrors, the glass chimney of a lamp lying under a dresser, and a heel mark on a magazine lying on a closet floor. Also, Sarah's blood-filled shoe was on J. B.'s side of the bed, as if picked up and moved. The ax, too, had been wiped off, as there were cloth fibers on it, and the killer had cleaned his hands on several items.

The investigating party went to the barn to see if the killer might have gone there. They saw a depression in some hay that was about the size and shape of a man who might have been lying in it. There was also a two-inch knothole that looked like a way to spy, because it afforded a view of the rear of the house.

Since the killer had covered most of the victim's heads or faces, there was reason to believe that he'd been acquainted with them, or that he believed if they opened their eyes and saw him, his visage might be impressed in the retina and thus detectable at autopsy. This was a common superstition. He had then drawn the curtains, possibly after he'd disabled everyone. Those windows without curtains he'd blacked out with clothing found inside the house. So he hadn't come prepared. An unexplained piece of this puzzle was the skirt he'd torn and draped over several mirrors. Was this some odd ritual?

Bloodhound handlers tried to track the killer, but he had a substantial head start. As leads ran dry, the potential for arresting someone dwindled to nothing. The crime was tentatively linked to a number of other axe murders of families around the country, but despite a psychotic confession from a seemingly psychotic minister, this mass homicide was never solved.

Former F.B.I. Profiler Robert Ressler discussed how he might have profiled the crime at the time. He believed the killer was probably a powerful man in his mid-to-late thirties, and that he was likely mentally ill with a borderline type of condition, but not full-blown psychosis.

Today, the restored house at Villisca is open for tours and ghost-hunting sleepovers.

The Steps

Death investigation involves reconstructing an incident, with the manner of death being the result of a homicide or suicide, an accident, natural causes or undetermined. A reconstruction is the process of determining the events and actions that occurred during the death event, including the examination and interpretation of physical and behavioral evidence. This process will follow the basic scientific method, which is the formulation of a hypothesis against which to systematically test the evidence. Experience, sound logic, and careful observation are necessary for an accurate reconstruction. The goal is to determine what happened, how it happened, when and where it happened, and who was (or was not) involved.

When a crime is initially discovered, a call goes out to authorities—generally via 911. A dispatcher notifies patrol units close by. Uniformed police arrive and decide whether they need other personnel (homicide or arson unit, for example). They note the time and write down pertinent observations, but refrain from touching or moving anything. If the perpetrator is present, the officer makes an arrest. Otherwise, the officer secures and controls the scene.

If an incident involves a body (or bodies), the coroner/medical examiner decides whether there is reason for an autopsy, or a postmortem medical examination for an official report. A partial autopsy examines only part of the body (for example, an injury to the head), while a selective autopsy may only involve a specific organ, such as the heart or brain.

Old and new injuries are noted, along with tattoos and scars. Trace evidence, such as hair and fibers, is collected from under the fingernails. The wrapping sheet, along with clothing and trace evidence, is sent to the forensic lab for analysis. Anything wet (like blood) must be air-dried and properly preserved.

The investigation might involve the search for a body when someone is missing and presumed dead, or the attempt to identify a found body and determine the cause and manner of death. It might also involve the identification and analysis of skeletal remains or an exhumation to look for something that might have been overlooked before burial.

An Exhumation

All deaths are treated as potential homicides until proven otherwise (although some incidents, like at Villisca, are obviously homicides). Similar to ghost hunting, there are several stages in the investigative process:

1. Preliminary analysis;
2. The primary evidence collection;
3. The analysis of evidence.

Another tool in a death investigation is an exhumation. No one could have compared DNA in 1882 when the outlaw Jesse James was shot and buried in the grave marked "Jesse W. James." Stories quickly spread that he had faked his death and escaped to live to old age, fathering children who had numerous descendants. With time, those stories were embellished.

To finally solve the mystery, Professor James Starrs brought DNA analysis and other tools of science to bear on the bones and teeth found inside the grave. In this case, Starrs used mitochondrial DNA analysis.

"In 1995," his team criminalist, Traci Brasse, says, "bone and teeth were recovered during an exhumation of the grave presumed to belong to Jesse James. While the bone was too degraded to recover DNA, reproducible mitochondrial DNA (mtDNA) sequencing was successful on DNA extracted from two molars, and this was compared to blood samples of two matrilineal descendants of Jesse James. It was found to be consistent with the maternal line. While mtDNA does not result in a conclusive identification, mtDNA sequencing did not exclude the exhumed remains to be those of Jesse James."

The results were incontrovertible: Jesse James had died from a gunshot wound in 1882. Thus, the ghost that reportedly wanders the James Farm where Jesse was buried could very well be his, still disturbed by the violence done to him.

Exhumations are warranted under the following conditions: when there is a dispute that must be cleared up, there are appropriate tools and techniques available, and a probability analysis can be done to decide if the remains will be in shape for the requisite analysis. This involves a variety of tasks, such as testing the soil pH and mineral content where the remains are buried, determining the method and depth of burial, knowing the time since burial (as well as any disturbances of the grave), and gathering climatic data (which falls under the science of forensic taphonomy).

The exhumation of Jesse James allowed new technology in forensic science to at least remove some of the doubt. It also negated the claims made by the supposed descendants of the infamous outlaw. The appearance of a ghost at a grave or murder site might inspire further digging.

Cops and Psychics

Paranormalists claim that there are two basic ways to gain information about a crime using paranormal methods. First, there's direct communication with the ghost of the victim (or a dead witness or perpetrator), using a medium or EVP technology. Second, the crime scene itself can provide residual paranormal evidence: perhaps a "replay" of the crime's noises or visuals could be gathered where they were imprinted by the emotional outbursts associated with a crime of passion. Again, a medium could tap into the surrounding subtle energy field and give clues to a paranormalist adept at collecting EVP, or a videographer or photographer using the correct scientific techniques could record what the environment releases.

Despite the fact that skeptics galore decry the use of psychics for anything but harmless entertainment, police departments around the country will call on certain psychics when all else fails. They've been doing that for over a century, and when forbidden to do so, they sometimes use unofficial means.

Former NYPD homicide cop, Vernon J. Geberth, wrote *Practical Homicide Investigation*, in which he includes a description of how to work with psychics. He's one of the few who admit to the practice, claiming that any technique that has proven successful should be considered again. His guidelines for cops are as follows:

- The psychic's performance will be tested by the results;
- The psychic will have a distinct method of operation;
- The psychic should be considered as an aid in developing clues;
- The police should provide all follow-up to information offered;
- Since there are no scientific guidelines, the police must determine whether the psychic's claims are legitimate or worth pursuing;
- Officers who cannot accept a psychic's work should not get involved, as their attitudes can block the psychic's effectiveness;
- The psychic should offer information not available to the public in publicized reports, as a way to prove his or her special insight;
- All conversations with the psychic should be taped.

The following is an example of investigators working with a psychic.

In November 1971, John List shot his wife, mother, and three children. Laying them out on sleeping bags in the ballroom of his New Jersey mansion, he turned on church music, left letters of confession to his minister, and took off. He said later that he'd fully expected to be caught immediately, but to his surprise, he managed to start life over in Colorado. He met another woman, got a job, joined a church, and took on a new identity.

Back in New Jersey, the case didn't die. The 13th anniversary of the monstrous crimes came and went, and suddenly there was renewed interest. A detective, Jeffrey Paul Hummel, was assigned to it in 1985. He worked on the Major Crimes Unit for the prosecutor's office in Union County, New Jersey, and he spent a lot of time learning about List.

List House

"Many in law enforcement presumed he was deceased," Hummel said. "However, I maintained he was alive because no evidence had ever surfaced to the contrary."

He was aware that the composite sketch of the age-progressed fugitive, published nationwide, had failed to turn up a good lead. Yet, because Hummel found the crime so repulsive, he was not about to give up. He decided to consult a psychic with a reputation for helping law enforcement with tough cases.

"In May of 1985," he said, "I became aware of a psychic living in Ocean County, New Jersey, identified as Elizabeth Lerner. Armed with crime scene photos, I spent about two hours with Ms. Lerner, who offered her feelings and impressions while touching the rear side of the photographs."

While Hummel received no concrete leads in tracking List down, he did get information that in retrospect was surprisingly accurate.

- Lerner said that List was alive and had not traveled by plane, as presumed from where he'd left his car, but by train or bus. (He had.)
- There was a new woman in his life and he had some connection with Baltimore, Maryland. (He had married his new wife in Baltimore.)
- He had fled to the southwest. (He went to Colorado.)
- There was some significance with Florida or Virginia. (List ended up in Virginia, which is where he was ultimately arrested.)

Ms. Lerner also made a prediction that gave Hummel something to do. List, she said, would visit the family gravesite on his birthday (September 17).

Hummel got permission to conduct surveillance in Westfield's Fairview Cemetery on September 16, 1985. Dressed in dark clothing, he prepared to sit outside all night on a hill overlooking the graves. Nothing happened that night, so he repeated his actions the following night, also to no avail. List did not arrive.

In fact, List was not caught until 1989, after *America's Most Wanted* aired the case and showed a bust of what the man might now look like. A former neighbor called in the tip that led the police right to him.

Although the psychic failed to offer a lead that would close the case, it was clear that she "saw" a few details that were accurate. A psychologist who assisted Frank Bender with the sculpture of List had surmised from logic that he would marry again and that he'd be fairly far afield from New Jersey, so these details weren't tough to guess.

However, the fact that List had returned to Baltimore to be married surprised a lot of people. Yet it's nevertheless troubling that the psychic felt so certain that List would visit the graves. He had never done so, he said, and had never intended to. Perhaps Lerner had said this because killers often do, so it was a guess that anyone could have made who knows about criminal behavior, but because the officers took her seriously, the suggestion did waste police resources.

Still, some officers do have experiences with the paranormal. A retired officer sent us this tale about a place where he grew up near Avondale, Pennsylvania, (site of a dramatic mine disaster in 1869 that claimed 110 lives).

"It was in that area," he said, "that I experienced my one and only ghost sighting. There was a large field across the street from my grandparents' house. The field was located on a hillside and the terrain was somewhat terraced. One summer night, I was playing in the field along with my older brother, sister, and three or four other kids. At one point someone pointed out a woman walking along the border of where the field met the woods. She was probably about fifty-yards away. For some reason he jokingly said, 'Hey, look, a ghost!' As everyone's attention turned towards the woman it was pretty clear she was wearing what appeared to be a long white dress.

"I'm not sure how all the pieces came together in the minds of everyone else, but I vividly remember realizing that her entire form was all the same color, sort of a darkish grey, but there was definitely a slight luminescence to her form. Someone then yelled, 'Hey, if you're a ghost, say something.'

"The figure stopped and her head turned towards us for a second before she disappeared into the woods. At this point it was as though there was a collective realization that it was a ghost and everyone sort of freaked out, but not in a fearful way, it was more of a 'Holy Shit' reaction.

"It was the type of experience that normally gets written off as the product of overactive teenage imaginations, but about a year later the guys who were with us that night were digging an underground fort in the same area of the field where we'd observed the woman walking. They unearthed a skeleton, and it was later determined to belong to a body that was buried long ago."

Special Knowledge

As part of the forensic anthropology department at the University of Tennessee at Knoxville (UT-K), a protected two-and-a-half-acre field has been dedicated to the study of decomposing human remains. Whatever they had been in life, in death these people have made a significant contribution to solving criminal cases. As they lay out, exposed to the elements, they provide information about what happens to bodies under such conditions. Although the Knoxville cops dubbed it the Body Farm, current faculty members refer to it simply as "the facility."

Forensic anthropology is the application of physical anthropology to the medico-legal process. That is, forensic anthropologists assist law enforcement investigators and medical examiners to identify human skeletal and decomposing remains, generally working in cooperation with pathologists and odontologists to estimate the age, sex, ancestry, stature, and unique bony features of the deceased. The Knoxville Anthropology Research Facility has made important contributions to estimating the time factors involved in suspicious deaths.

"Before our work," says founder Bill Bass, "no one had ever established a time line. There are a lot of factors that can affect how a body decomposes, but we found that the major two are climate and insects. When a person dies, the body begins to decay immediately and the enzymes in the digestive system begin to eat the tissue. You putrefy, and this gives off a smell. The first of the critters to be attracted to a decaying body are the blowflies. They come along and lay their eggs, which hatch into maggots. The maggots then eat the decaying tissue in a fairly predictable way." Measuring and recording this information gave the Body Farm its *raison d'être*.

Body Farm

The science of forensic taphonomy is the discovery, recovery, and analysis of human remains in a context that has legal ramifications. This discipline deals with the complex factors involved in the history after death of physical remains and the ways in which death-related processes have affected them. Different climates will affect decomposition rates, with cool temperatures having a greater preservative effect and thus a longer period for decomposing.

To get a useful taphonomic reading requires the team effort of professionals from different disciplines, including biology, entomology, anthropology, and pathology, as well as botany and geology. It might even involve climatology—an analysis of the weather patterns, or an archaeological examination of soil layers in a grave.

Body Farm Bones

A facility at Texas State University that takes its cue from the Body Farm has studied the behavior of vultures. Experienced investigators would normally have interpreted the absence of flesh and the condition of bones for remains found in a field, for example, as evidence that they had been there for six months, possibly a year. Now the vulture study, conducted on 26 acres, is calling into question many of the benchmarks on which detectives have long relied.

Scientists set up a motion-sensing camera that captured the vultures jumping up and down on the remains, breaking some of the ribs, which investigators might also misinterpret as trauma suffered during a beating.

Researchers there have been monitoring a half-dozen other corpses in various stages of decomposition. The initial surprise was that it took vultures 37 days to find a body intentionally placed out for them. Researchers visited the site daily and checked the camera for any activity. Then a graduate student working on another project at the site alerted them to the vultures' arrival and swift work on the corpse.

Besides a specific focus on death, responders must follow other types of crime scene protocols for reconstruction of an incident. This will take us back to the paranormal.

Incident Reconstruction

Professor John Allison is a forensic chemist. When a writer acquaintance told him a strange story, he believed it was an opportune moment for his expertise.

The writer's longtime friend had died, and almost at once, strange things began happening in the writer's home. The deceased friend—whom we'll call F. A.—had been involved for most of his life in the horror industry. In fact, his home had been a veritable museum of horror films and books. F. A. had said that he'd offer a sign after he died that he was still "around." The writer wondered if this could be happening.

One of the oddest incidents occurred just after the writer printed out a document that contained F. A.'s name. He left the room and returned to discover that a line in the document had been crossed out, obliterating the name. No one else was home at the time and there was no liquid source anywhere near the document that would explain this kind of obliteration. The writer was baffled, so he brought the problem to Allison.

Intrigued, Allison examined the paper. The obliteration was a bluish substance on top of black printer's ink. He tried a number of tests on the paper, but he could not recreate the obliteration. He did find foreign elements, so he applied laser desorption mass spectrometry. However, no source in the writer's home matched the foreign elements.

During the period in which the document was undergoing this examination, several odd things occurred in the writer's home, including unwound clocks chiming at the moment the writer was telling someone what had occurred with the document. However, despite the application of sophisticated tests, the mystery remained unsolved. If F. A. was around, he apparently could not make his presence more clearly known.

The logic of reconstruction consists of scientific observation, hypothesis formation, and the elimination of possibilities through testing. No conclusion that provided a definitive resolution was reached in this case. It was presented to forensic scientists at a conference to generate more ideas for tests, but no one else had ideas.

Locard's Exchange Principle is often cited in forensics publications, "Every contact leaves a trace." This notion is applied to crime scenes. The perpetrator(s) will bring something into the scene and take away some trace of the scene on his (or their) person(s). In the cyber world, the perpetrator may or may not come in physical contact with the crime scene, so this brings a new facet to the analysis.

At the 2012 meetings of the American Academy of Forensic Sciences, Rod Englert, an expert on blood spatter pattern analysis, gave a presentation on his analysis of the Civil War-era death of Jennie Wade in Gettysburg, Pennsylvania. Since Mark had done a paranormal investigation, it was a good opportunity to bring together the results of two different, but complementary approaches.

Jennie Wade was the only civilian killed in the infamous battle of Gettysburg. Thousands of tourists every year tramp through the death house, now a museum, and read the theory about who'd shot her. Englert assured Katherine that the evidence contradicts the way it's told.

General Robert E. Lee, for the South, and General George Meade, for the North, faced off for what Lee hoped would be the definitive follow-up victory to his army's string of recent victories. He'd penetrated Pennsylvania, so Meade maneuvered his army to protect Washington, D. C. An accidental initial clash resulted in a Union defeat and they were driven through the small, south-central Pennsylvania town of Gettysburg. The next two days of battle occurred south of the town. This epic three-day clash in early July 1863, resulted in a Union victory with a combined 51,000 military causalities, the bloodiest battle ever fought on American soil. On July 3, someone shot civilian Jennie Wade.

As the legend goes, during a skirmish a Confederate sharpshooter stationed in the Farnsworth House's attic inadvertently killed Jennie. The day before her death, she'd been making and handing out bread to hungry soldiers and early on the morning of July 3, she'd decided to make more, so she was kneading the dough in the kitchen of her sister's brick house. The bullet that killed her penetrated an exterior door on the north side, slammed through another interior door, and struck Jennie in the back. She died quickly. This is actually a tragic love story because the 20-year-old girl was engaged to a Union solder. Her beau had no idea his girl was dead, because he himself had been mortally wounded as the two armies fought on their way to Gettysburg.

So, Englert traveled to Gettysburg in 1989. He went to the museum, looked at the bullet holes that had splintered the doors, then read the theory that the bullet had been shot from inside the Farnsworth House. He felt unsettled: his training told him this couldn't be right.

In 2003, he returned to perform a full-scale bullet trajectory analysis. With permission, he ran a string from the first hole through the second one to the dough tray, and realized from measurements that the second hole was more than three inches higher than the first. This had been no downward trajectory and his findings "cast doubt on the theory that the sniper who fired it was in a building. He would have been positioned low and firing upward."

Englert's next step was to learn the lay of the land in 1863, so he looked for maps and descriptions, as well as military records of who had been stationed where. He believed the bullet had probably come from a field not a building, and from farther away. Englert then staged a re-enactment. He had an actress dress in period costume, including the type of corset Jennie had been wearing, to see exactly how the bullet would have hit her under the shoulder blade. He concluded that the original story was incorrect.

CSI

When officers arrive at a crime scene, they determine what other investigators will be needed (the homicide or arson unit, for example). Officers note whether there are any distinct odors, the lights are on or off, the blinds are drawn, mail or newspapers are piled up, or food is spoiled. If someone at the scene is attempting to clean it up, that person must be stopped.

Officers control the scene by marking the perimeter with tape or a clearly marked barrier, and by keeping everyone clear of the defined area. This prevents the destruction of evidence. One of the most difficult aspects of controlling a scene is defining its boundaries. If there's been a murder, the crime scene could extend to other rooms where the killer left traces of his or her presence, out into a hallway, and even into a neighborhood.

The first twenty-four hour period after a crime is considered the most crucial, because the evidence is relatively undisturbed and witnesses have better memories. The suspect's trail is still fresh. As evidence is collected, categorized and sent to the proper technicians or scientists for analysis, investigators gather to discuss the logical order of events. This is done to generate leads and to evaluate the perpetrator(s).

Criminalists with special education and training include:

- Anthropology—examines bones to help determine identity and may also get involved in time of death issues, as well as forensic art.
- Ballistics—has knowledge about the functioning of firearms and bullet projectiles.
- Chemist/Trace expert—studies the molecular component of pieces of evidence like glass, paint chips, fibers, and dyes. Also does toxicology.
- Dactyloscopy—analyzes fingerprints.
- Entomology—studies the developmental stages of insects to help establish time of death or body dumpsites.
- Geology—analyzes soil content to provide information about where a body may have been.
- Mental health experts/criminologist/profiler—helps to determine how the evidence is to be interpreted by analyzing potential motives and criminal behavior from a crime scene. They can also predict what a serial offender might do, narrow down identifying characteristics, and explain puzzling aspects of a crime.
- Odontologist/dentist—examines teeth impressions, bite marks, and dental formation for identification.
- Serologist—analyzes body serums like blood, semen, and saliva, and may offer information about DNA and blood pattern analysis.

In jurisdictions that have funding for full facilities, physical evidence is reserved for the crime scene technicians who are trained in how to collect it, and for the criminalists, "identification technicians," or forensic scientists who do the analyses.

Crime scene personnel look for things that should not be there—foreign elements that seem out of place. They know that people routinely shed hairs and fibers, and that many things can be used as weapons. They will have various duties, including taking notes, evaluating the scene, sketching it, photographing it, finding and collecting physical evidence for analysis, using different types of equipment, and preparing detailed reports. Sometimes they will take portable processing equipment to the scene, where they will work with the evidence.

They must also be prepared to testify in court about what they write in evidence reports. Essentially they're looking for:

- Fingerprints;
- Impressions from tools, shoes, car tires, fabric, and teeth;
- Body fluids like semen, blood, and saliva;
- Other biological evidence such as hair, fingernail scrapings, and body tissue;
- Trace evidence such as glass, plant spoors, fibers, paint chips, gunshot residue, and accelerant;
- Weapons or the evidence of them, such as shell casings;
- Questioned documents, which include forged checks, fake suicide notes, and ransom notes;
- Special evidence in cases of arson or explosions.

Reconstruction

Crime scene reconstruction uses scientific methods, physical and testimonial evidence, and different types of logical and inventive reasoning to determine the sequence of events at a given time and place. It generally takes a lot of work to reveal how the crime occurred and who was involved.

The initial step is to get briefed by the first responding officers and make a summary of statements from anyone involved. After this, they do a careful walk-through, observing everything, avoiding evidence contamination, and making preliminary conjectures. Experienced investigators are aware that appearances can be deceiving, so they withhold judgment until the facts are in.

Paranormal investigators can use these steps as guidelines for their investigations. The basic steps in a reconstruction are:

1. Observe everything;
2. Recognize evidence (note anything out of place, suspicious, or obvious);
3. Document it with notes, diagrams, and photos;
4. Collect it and place markers where it was found;
5. Evaluate it for as much information as possible;
6. Devise a working hypothesis of how the incident occurred;

7. Test the hypothesis against the evidence, often by simulating what is assumed to have happened to see how it plays out;

8. Use everything available to reconstruct the action at the scene and write up a report.

Inexperienced investigators (like some ghost hunters), look for evidence to support a hypothesis, which is quite easy to do, rather than adequately testing a hypothesis before accepting it. Thus, they get tunnel vision, which means they might make false claims and also miss evidence that they cannot go back and recover.

Investigators are vulnerable to several mental errors, most notably threshold diagnosis and assumptions from familiarity (also called gut instinct). So are ghost hunters. This derives from what psychologists call *heuristics*, or mental shortcuts. Because we have limited mental capacity, we become cognitive misers. We use shortcuts to reduce complex information into simple rules-of-thumb.

However, because heuristics form automatically and without thoughtful consideration they can cause errors. Thus, they can influence poor decisions that negatively impact people's lives. They can hinder—even damage—a criminal investigation.

Our brain encodes our experiences to produce expectations. Research reveals, for example, that exposing subjects to a specific context will influence their interpretation of an ambiguous stimulus. If they see numbers before seeing a symbol that looks like both a 'B' and the number 13, they see 13; if they're shown letters first, they see a 'B'. Contexts influence our readiness to perceive something in accordance with our expectations. We selectively attend to certain aspects of a stimulus while failing to process others.

Analysis of paranormal evidence as well is subject to a phenomenon of the brain called apophenia. The visual area of the brain is set up, when confronted with partial data, to "connect the dots" or fill in the blanks to complete the identification of an external stimulus. It's why people will pay thousands of dollars on e-Bay for the "image" of the Virgin Mary on a grilled cheese sandwich. It is also the reason people will see ghostly faces in the matrix of leaves from a battlefield photo.

Apophenia can apply to audio evidence, too. During EVP analysis, researchers must be careful not to hear the answer to the question asked—sometimes the EVP is not an answer but some other words not related to the question at all. In analyzing paranormal evidence, experienced researchers will try to avoid influencing others. For example, they won't share their original impressions of what they see or hear—sometimes even writing their impressions down—until they discover what others experienced.

Detective Kim Rossmo studied how certain cognitive processes affect investigations. He found that recall is more consistent with personal beliefs than with facts, especially as it supports a formulated hypothesis, and contradictory information is generally ignored. Rossmo points out that clear and rational thinking is not automatic and the human brain is not wired to deal effectively with uncertainty. The result of these pressures can be a quick threshold diagnosis, which limits the focus.

Gregg McCrary agrees with Rossmo. He recognizes that there are many things that are based on personal experience. "It can be vulnerable to error," he said, "but it's also your area of expertise, your shortcut in getting to the right place."

This is one reason why paranormal investigations, if at all possible, should be done during the daylight hours. Just how the senses are skewed and rational thought is affected when "hunting ghosts" in the dark can only be imagined. (We have proof from cognitive research that as conditions for visual input deteriorate, the brain relies more strongly on expectation to process the data.)

Rossmo states that some information goes through rational channels and some goes through emotional, or intuitive, channels. Intuition, he says, is aligned with automatic, subconscious judgment. It is rapid and its conclusions form without benefit of analysis. Thus, it is highly vulnerable to error. Although reasoning is slower, it opens the mind to a greater range of factors and the result is more reliable. In other words, what feels right is not necessarily what *is* right.

One influencing factor is the accessibility from memory of specific social constructs. One study involving detectives provided them with a scenario in which various murder suspects looked more or less guilty, based on social stereotypes. The detectives then received ambiguous evidence from witness statements. In the condition in which a suspect looked guilty, the detectives tended to interpret the ambiguous evidence toward guilt.

In addition, the structure of a story can facilitate a mental transition from specific details to a summary of abstractions, otherwise known as the "gist" of a story. Researchers found that mock jurors were more strongly influenced by evidence presented in story form than as a set of facts. In addition, evidence presented ambiguously received a spin in the direction of the story frame.

Complex tasks such as a criminal investigation should be undertaken carefully, with eyes and mind open. Cognitive biases present a persistent challenge for criminal investigators. It is important to minimize their influence. As heuristics reduce complexity, they can introduce error. Since detectives have considerable discretion in making investigative decisions, being aware of these perceptual quirks can remind them to exercise caution about quick decisions, even if—and *especially* if—those decisions feel "right." Paranormalists have similar issues.

When a psychic is employed, information about the site should be limited. The fact that it had been the scene of a crime should be withheld if at all possible. This is why a paranormal technique like remote viewing—which we'll discuss later—would be a valuable tool in a paranormal investigation of a crime scene.

Behavioral Evidence

While crime scene units focus on physical evidence, some psychology is always involved, and at times investigators must consider that before drawing conclusions about the physical evidence.

Among the tools of crime investigation is the art of behavioral profiling, which assists investigators to narrow the pool of suspects by devising a portrait from evidence at a crime scene of what the offender was probably like.

Among the first profiles ever done was Thomas Bond's speculative description of the type of person who was committing the prostitute murders attributed to Jack the Ripper. At the same time, a psychic offered his impressions, and it's interesting to compare the two approaches.

Some F.B.I. profilers have offered profiles of famous crimes that also have paranormal associations; thus once again, we can use one approach to fill in gaps from the other. What former F.B.I. profiler John Douglas said about the double homicide at Lizzie Borden's house, for example, can help us understand the hauntings that reportedly occur there. (We'll go into more detail about this case in a later chapter.)

So, let's look at a case that a psychic and a profiler separately examined. It involved a serial killer.

Dorothy Allison, an American psychic famous for locating missing persons, reportedly predicted the murders of two teenage girls before the incidents occurred. In March 1991, young Melanie Hall disappeared from her home in Niagara Falls, Canada. Police called Dorothy Allison and she asked for a photograph of the girl and a small item of the girl's property. With the girl's date and hour of birth, she made an astrological chart. She envisioned a girl dismembered and her various parts encased in cement. One leg, she said, would be "popping out."

But there had been no such discovery. Allison agreed to come to the area, and as she drove with police past a lake, she had a strong impression of a girl to whom something had happened—it was still the same vision.

Two months later, on June 15, 1991, 14-year-old Leslie Mahaffy turned up missing from Burlington, which was halfway between Scarborough in Toronto and Niagara Falls. After attending a memorial service for a schoolmate killed in a car accident, she had gone to a store. Then she went home late in the company of a male friend, but found the doors locked. No one responded to her knocking. Her friend went home, and Leslie disappeared.

Two weeks later on the evening of June 29, Leslie's dismembered body was found along the shore of Lake Gibson in St. Catharines, a town close to Niagara Falls and about thirty miles east from where she had lived. Her body had been cut into separate pieces and sealed into seven concrete blocks. These blocks were pulled from the water. One block contained a foot and thigh, and a second block contained a severed foot and a calf. Oddly, the block containing her head was spray-painted black. The next evening in another area across the lake, a fisherman stumbled across the missing torso.

Leslie was not the girl that had made police contact Allison, but Allison's vision corresponded quite specifically with this incident. The police developed no leads, so they called Allison again. She couldn't supply anything to help, but she told them that the body of another victim would soon be found, within a week. This girl would be strangled and she would be found underneath some brush, where one could hear trickling water.

Even as she said it, the girl was already missing. On April 16, 1992, honor student Kristen French, 15, began her daily walk home from Holy Cross secondary school in St. Catharines. Her half-mile walk home along the busy Linwell Road took about fifteen minutes, and a friend driving by had seen her there at 2:50 P.M., near Grace Lutheran Church. Nevertheless, she never made it home that afternoon.

The Niagara Regional Police acted quickly. Within 24 hours, they had called the press, assigned a team, and searched both sides of Linwell Road from Kristen's school to her home. Based upon the thorough neighborhood investigation, they developed several witnesses to Kristin French's abduction. Each had observed different aspects, and together they provided a good account of what had happened. It seemed that a car had slowed and the driver had spoken to the girl. He had an accomplice, who grabbed Kristin and forced her into the car.

On April 30, Kristen's body was found unclothed and lying on its side on Number One side road in Burlington. Her hair had been cut short and she was partly covered with branches, leaves and debris, near a culvert. It was clear from extensive bruising—especially on her face—that she had been repeatedly assaulted and then strangled or asphyxiated.

Gregg McCrary had come into the case a few years earlier, when the perpetrator was still just a rapist—the Scarborough Rapist. He had predicted that the brutal rapist would soon turn to murder. When this occurred, he worked with the Toronto police on a profile.

"This is the only time I know of where someone profiled the same unknown offender twice," he said. "First it was for a series of rapes. Then it was for a series of murders of young women. We could see from the level of sadism that he would finally turn to murder, and he did."

Ultimately, good police work solved the case. A DNA test identified Paul Bernardo as a serial rapist who had prowled the area, and his wife, Karla Homolka, had gone to the police on a complaint of spousal abuse. Under pressure, she turned him in as the killer of the two girls—and, additionally, of her own sister. After she cut a plea deal, police learned that Karla had been fully part of each of these horrendous crimes.

Dorothy Allison had predicted the finding of Leslie Mahaffy before she was missing, and even had she learned about Kristin French's abduction—it had been international news—she could not have known in advance the murder method or details about the dumpsite. She got them right.

Michael Dennett, who writes for *The Skeptical Inquirer*, tried looking into Allison's impressive record of "hits." When he requested police commendations that would spell out just how she had helped to solve a crime, he says that her publicist assured him that he could send hundreds, but he sent only three. Of these, only one offered the information Dennett was seeking, but the case failed to pan out.

"No case identified in the many magazine articles, newspaper clippings or in her book," Dennett says, "provide independent, unambiguous verification that Allison's participation resulted in her finding a body." For the most part, he discovered, the police who were impressed with her had fit their facts into her scenario afterward.

Dennett checked with police officers with whom Allison had worked and learned that some had experienced her making wrong guesses and wasting their resources for as long as a week. But then she would request a letter of commendation for her files. One officer apparently told Dennett that when Allison was denied this letter in a specific case of a missing girl, she offered to pay them for it. Allison apparently then claimed credit for solving the crime, so the cop went public with his part of the tale.

"I give them what I've got," Allison said in her defense, "and they do what they want with it." She never did see the original missing girl in the Canadian case, and though a killer confessed to murdering her, Allison's clues failed to send authorities to the body. It was never found.

McCrary's profile helped in the Kristin French case, however. It was televised and the killers were watching. Abused by Bernardo and afraid that investigators were closing in, Karla Homolka turned him in and orchestrated a deal. For her cooperation and a plea of guilty to two counts of manslaughter, she was sentenced to two concurrent twelve-year terms.

The task force also relied on behavioral analysis, supplied by Gregg McCrary, to get a search warrant to find tapes of the sexual torture sessions they believed were in Bernardo's home. Although they failed to locate these tapes, they did convince a judge that Bernardo was a dangerous individual. He was convicted of two murders and numerous sexual assaults, getting life in prison. He is still suspected in other assaults and murders. (The tapes eventually turned up in the hands of Bernardo's attorney.)

We asked Gregg McCrary what he would have done with the information from Allison, had he heard her accurately describe the Mahaffy murder.

"I would want to find out if she really nailed it like she says," he told us. "If I can establish that she made this call before it happened, I'd want to talk to her. I'd want to know what she saw and anything else she was getting on this. I want to get as much information as I can. You'll take crap for talking to a psychic, but we didn't have anything else. It was a paramount public safety issue. You can't leave any stone unturned."

The Psychological Autopsy

Besides profiling, there's another tool in forensic psychology that can assist: a psychological autopsy. In death certifications, there are three important matters: the cause, mechanism and manner of death. The cause is an instrument or physical agent used to bring about death (a bullet, for example), the mechanism is the pathological agent in the body that resulted in the death (excessive bleeding), and the manner of death is considered to be natural, accidental, homicide or suicide. Sometimes the manner isn't clear, so the death is classified as "undetermined."

In such cases, a psychological autopsy might assist the coroner or medical examiner in clearing up the mystery. It involves discovering the state of mind of the victim preceding death. A close examination of the death scene may indicate degree of intent and lethality—a secluded place and the use of a gun indicating a higher degree than using slow-acting pills in a place where the victim is likely to be discovered.

Psychological autopsies are often done on famous cases where certain factors make the death more complex than the official determination admits. Marilyn Monroe's suicide, for example, is still questioned today because there were too many odd incidents involving other people, as well as her own erratic state of mind. In cases where the deceased seems to appear as a ghost, as Monroe reportedly has, perhaps there's a reason. In any event, a psychological autopsy is a forensic tool that could clear up some of the ambiguity surrounding such deaths.

In addition to theorizing on how a site can be haunted, paranormalists have developed a similar protocol for evaluating why the surviving spirit of a person might remain at a site. In ghost hunting, some of the reasons postulated include: unfinished business; an unexpected death; a youthful death; a violent demise; concern for the living; a death so sudden that they don't know that they're dead; fear of final judgment; and concern that someone among the living is grieving too long. Violent crimes and sudden deaths appear to show up most often in our ghost lore.

Visual and Audio

In Amityville, New York, six members of an affluent family were shot to death in their beds one night. Ronald "Butch" DeFeo, Jr., 23, the only survivor, called it in. At first he threw blame on organized crime, but his story fell apart. He became the prime suspect and finally admitted his cold-blooded act.

Amityville House

On November 13, 1974, at approximately 3:00 A.M., Butch took a .35-caliber lever-action Marlin rifle and murdered his father, mother, two sisters, and two brothers. The youngest was nine. DeFeo then removed his clothing, bathed, and redressed. He cleaned up the crime scene, picked up cartridges and stuffed them along with his bloody clothing into a pillowcase. This "package" he dropped into a sewer on his way to work and tossed the rifle into a canal.

To a psychiatrist, DeFeo described blackouts he'd experienced in which he did things he could not recall. Eventually he said the murders were done in self-defense during a violent family argument. But then he said his sister had done it with his gun. Finally, he claimed that the police had coerced a false confession out of him. Ultimately he said that he had killed because he was God, and he pleaded not guilty by reason of insanity.

85

Dr. Daniel Schwartz, a psychiatrist, affirmed the delusions and DeFeo's paranoid belief that his family had it in for him. Schwartz stated that he'd acted out against them while in a psychotic state, so he could not be held responsible. As evidence of dissociation, Schwartz relied on DeFeo's claim that he had not heard the gun firing. In addition, his attempt to hide the evidence was irrational.

The prosecutor also hired a psychiatrist, Dr. Harold Zolan. He diagnosed antisocial personality disorder. Butch knew right from wrong and appreciated the consequences of his act. That's why he'd hidden the evidence that linked him to the crimes.

The house was sold and it ended up as the setting for another fraud, *The Amityville Horror*, a book and movie based on the idea that the house had been built on an Indian burial ground (or a place where the Shinnecocks kept their insane) and the restless spirits had caused anyone who lived there to become insanely violent. DeFeo had just been one of them, a pawn in the hands of an evil spirit.

George and Kathy Lutz moved into the house, which still had a lot of the DeFeo's furniture, and were soon under attack. George supposedly morphed into DeFeo and Kathy had persistent nightmares about the DeFeo family murders. A priest who came to bless the house supposedly grew quite ill.

An attorney working with the Lutzes later claimed in print that they'd all devised the scheme together over drinks, but he sued them for money owed and they sued him for what he'd said, so no one quite knew what to make of the whole affair. Several ghost hunters affirmed that the place was indeed haunted by evil entities, but skeptics pointed to the numerous errors in the story and the fact that all of the families who moved in after the Lutzes had experienced no negative effects.

It seems that whether one thinks this house is haunted or not is the deciding factor on how various incidents get reported. Ghost hunters have gone over this property with various tools of the trade, from psychics to séances to photography. No one has yet used sophisticated forensic tools to try to record and analyze voices.

Among the most important tools in both paranormal and forensic investigation is photography.

Photography

Ghost hunting involves video and still photography of all types, always searching for the best medium for recording elusive phenomena. Similarly, forensic photographers work hard on choosing the best equipment and techniques, since lighting and difficult conditions challenge them to get the best possible reproductions of potential evidence. Crime scene photographers tend to follow certain protocols:

1. They use both black-and-white and various types of color print film (some may use digital cameras for ready access to computer enhancement).
2. They use different types of lenses, normal and wide angle, as well as lenses for close-up work; they may also need a telephoto lens for distances.
3. They bring extension flashes and other supplementary lighting to achieve crisper detail and depth photography.
4. They use a tripod to keep shots steady.
5. They use a photograph log to keep track of each shot.
6. They bring filters for better depth.
7. They include different types of scales in the photos for accurately measuring things like shoe imprints.
8. They take at least two photos of each shot, in case one is blurred.

The procedure for crime scene photographers is to first walk through the scene to get perspective (taking care not to move, touch, or step on anything). They then discuss with the investigating officers what should be photographed in greater detail. There's little doubt that what's at stake—solving a case—inspires them to keep improving their craft, so anyone, including ghost hunters, can benefit from following their practices.

An important skill involved in forensic photography is the ability to determine when a photo has been faked. One method uses the direction of the light source vs. shadow effects. Analysis of a subject's eyes can also produce results, as can the pixel count of cloned areas (lifted from another photo) and "camera fingerprints."

Since many ghost images have been faked, using tips we provide from forensic analysts can help weed out fraud.

With 3-D laser scanning and 360° panoramic digital photography, animations of crime scenes can be constructed for improved brainstorming about incident reconstruction. The same can be done for paranormal incidents where contained scenes are available. Alternative light sources, which assist with photography, are used to find biological fluids, footprints, and other impressions not readily visible. This could be useful to ghost hunters, not just to expose fraud but also to locate paranormal evidence.

Investigators can experience difficulty when trying to get accurate measurements of a scene in order to reconstruct it into a scaled diagram that can be used as a 2-D map or 3-D model. Recent innovations involve color-coded targets for camera orientation on such things as blood spatter, bullet trajectory, and incident chronology. The investigator needs a digital camera, close-range photogramatry software, clear targets for marking, a laser rangefinder, and a computer program that diagrams. The targets are made from red reflective material, and the software measures the distances among them, helping to scale the unit in question to the right dimensions. If the model is sufficiently detailed, the investigator can create a "walk-through movie" of the scene replica.

No crime scene search is complete without using an alternative light source (ALS). A fluorescent light will illuminate things like latent fingerprints, trace evidence, and biological stains not seen with the naked eye. An ALS transmits light through a filter, or series of filters, to pass a specific wavelength through a delivery device. An ALS is monochromatic, because all of the transmitted light has the same wavelength and frequency. When the ALS is shone on items that could become evidence, and the light is absorbed and re-emitted, it can produce a temporary fluorescence or a longer lasting phosphorescence (persistent glow). Whether or not people actually get "slimed" during ghost hunting, paranormal incidents have left traces, and an ALS might help show them more clearly.

Currently, paranormal investigators are encouraged to always take more than just one photo of a suspected haunted site. One theory is that ghostly phenomena may exist in a frequency not perceptible to the normal human eye. (Film or video is recorded at 30 frames per second which is what the eye can comfortably see; if the frequency is faster, like the speed of a fan or airplane propeller, the object disappears, possibly explaining why ghosts are often invisible.) Multiple photos may just happen to pick up an entity appearing. Paranormal investigators are experimenting with ultra-violet and infrared strobes to see if they can match the frequency of the entities they're attempting to capture.

Forensic Acoustics/Phonetic Science

Speech or noise recognition expertise deals in acoustic evidence and involves training in linguistic analysis, philology, human anatomy, decoding procedures, phonetics, and even physics. Phonetics is about speech production, transmission, and perception. Such professionals must train their ear to make fine distinctions, as well as learn to understand how sounds or voiceprints are displayed visually as a spectrograph. Phonetic science involves speech enhancement and decoding, tape authentication, speech analysis, and the identification of a speaker. Adding acoustic analysis broadens the discipline to include analyzing such things as gunshots, the impact of machines in an accident, and musical sounds.

Bell Telephone Laboratories developed voiceprint technology in 1941, for communication information during World War II. It was first used in a forensic context in the early 1960s for bomb threats against major airlines.

Senior Bell Labs employee Lawrence G. Kersta was a physicist with extensive experience. Having analyzing over 50,000 voices, he believed the technique was 99.65% accurate. He was one of the first people to recognize that qualities unique to each person's voice can be processed and charted on a graph, because the physical vocal mechanisms create differences from one person to another. The size and shape of the vocal cavity, tongue, and nasal cavities contribute, as well as how a subject coordinates his or her lips, jaw, tongue, and soft palate to make speech. Kersta insisted that voices remain stable over a lifetime, although this notion initially remained theoretical.

Now, examiners use software that takes the recording in question, plus a recording of a known person's voice, and compares the two using three tests. Usually, the recording in question has to be at least seven seconds long.

The software does a spectrograph analysis, an average pitch analysis, and a statistical analysis involving a database of millions of voices. You run the two samples through the program, which then provides a percentage from 0–100% of the likelihood that they are the same. To call two samples a match requires at least 60%. The analyst then relies on his judgment to compare an accent, syntax and breathing patterns in the recordings, which the program does not analyze.

Voice and noise analyses are done on a sound spectrograph. The human vocal column begins in the vocal folds and ends at the lips. The vocal folds provide a closed end, making the vocal column a resonator, with vocal fold tension determining the frequency of the vibrations. As a sound is produced, those harmonics nearest the vocal column's resonant frequency increase in amplitude. The spectrograph then converts the sound into a visual graphic display, a voiceprint.

With an analog spectrograph, a magnetic high-quality tape is placed on a scanning drum, which holds a measured segment of tape time. As the drum revolves, an electronic filter allows a specified band of frequencies to get through, and these are translated into electrical energy. A stylus records the energy signature onto special paper. As the process continues, the filter moves into increasingly higher frequencies and the stylus records the intensity levels of each range. The horizontal axis on a voiceprint registers how high or low a voice is. The vertical axis is the frequency. The degree of darkness within each region on the graph illustrates intensity or volume.

For most forensic purposes, comparisons are made between known and questioned samples. When sufficient similarity exists between the patterns that both voice samples make on the graph, they have a "high probability" of originating from the same person. The highest standard for testifying in court requires the identification of similarities among twenty distinct speech sounds.

The skills involved in aural and visual voice interpretation include critical and sensitive listening, an ability to check for tape tampering, experience reading magnetic tapes, an ability to operate the spectrograph equipment, and the ability to work with an investigative team.

All studies on spectrographic accuracy show that properly trained experts who use standard aural and visual procedures get highly accurate results. Those who do the recordings for analysis must also be competent to operate the recording device, because the quality of the tape has great bearing on the interpreter's results.

Speech enhancement and decoding involves the elimination of interference in order to clarify the questioned speech or sound. Filtering tools are used for this procedure, as well as repeated listening to every detail. If the voice is anonymous, such as with a bomb threat or ransom demand, the voice recording can still offer information about the caller, such as age, race, gender and country (or region) of origin. In addition, background noises that occur during the call can be isolated and subject to the process of identification. If a suspect is developed, this person's voice can be recorded and compared to the questioned sample.

In addition to voices, other types of sounds can be key factors in a forensic investigation. In 2008, acoustic analysis by experts Philip Van Praag and Robert Joling turned up new evidence in the assassination of Senator Robert F. Kennedy on June 5, 1968, at the Ambassador Hotel in California. Although Sirhan Sirhan did lift a pistol and take several shots at Kennedy, the new theory indicates that not only did Sirhan possibly conspire with someone else, he did not actually make the fatal wounds.

Kennedy and his entourage went through the hotel's pantry area, and after he shook hands with two of the staff, he was hit four times. Three bullets entered his body, including one into his brain, and one lodged in a shoulder pad on his suit. He was removed to a hospital, where he died the next day.

Sirhan, a Palestinian refugee, was arrested and taken into custody. He admitted he had shot Kennedy and claimed it was for the cause of exploited people. Witnesses who had wrestled with him confirmed that he was the shooter. Yet Sirhan had been in front of

Kennedy and the autopsy indicated that the bullets that hit Kennedy had come from behind him and were shot at close range. Sirhan had only eight bullets in his revolver, but fourteen bullets were lodged in walls around the room or in other people (who all survived).

A journalist had been recording Kennedy's appearance and his recorder was still running during the shooting incident, so a tape was available for analysis. Joling and van Praag went to work. The recording quality was poor, but during the course of five seconds, they were able to count thirteen separate shots.

Two pairs of double shots occurred so close in time it was impossible for a single shooter to have gotten them off, even an expert (which they reconstructed). Five of the shots had unusual acoustic characteristics, and the scientists proposed that they came from a different type of gun, pointed at a different angle. This state-of-the-art analysis might eventually inspire a new investigation, clearing Sirhan and implicating someone else—perhaps someone in Kennedy's entourage.

The ability to crystalize subtle sounds for improved clarity so many years later suggested that paranormalists could use the technology for EVP. Recordings of EVP might be the most unimpeachable data able to be collected in a paranormal investigation, due to the fact that a recorder is an objective machine. Even the Vatican has ruled that EVP is recorded on an objective device that merely collects the voices from wherever they come.

Currently, paranormalists who gather EVP use computer programs to analyze their samples. Even the most cost-effective downloads offer numerous sophisticated noise "washing" tools and graphic analysis for visual study. Many of the techniques and science used in forensics could be applied to EVP analysis, such as speech enhancement and voice identification, although if EVP is truly electronic in nature, with no larynx, tongue or mouth cavity (all of which have decomposed) the voice of the dead person might bear little likeness to his voice when he was alive.

Dr. Renato Orso of Turin, Italy, used a device called a sonograph in identifying EVP. The sonograph is so reliable, it is recognized in court proceedings in Italy. Whether American jurists can be persuaded to allow EVP evidence into the courtroom remains to be determined in the future.

Unique Identifiers

During the Depression years when banks were failing right and left, Americans glamorized a handful of bank robbers. They followed the exploits of these criminals in newspapers as if reading a serialized thriller, cheering for them and criticizing the police. J. Edgar Hoover, head of the F.B.I., was outraged, especially by John Dillinger's grandiose attacks during the mid-1930s on Chicago-area banks. Hoover dubbed him "Public Enemy Number One."

Arrested once and heavily guarded in an "escape-proof" prison, Dillinger used a fake gun to escape. Then he crossed the state line into Indiana and went into hiding. The F.B.I. closed in and Dillinger grew nervous. Knowing that fingerprints identified the corpses of other criminals, and that prints left at a crime scene could incriminate him, he devised a plan. He paid a team of plastic surgeons to alter his face and used acid to burn off his fingerprints. He nearly died under the botched anesthesia, but finally the operation was finished. His fingerprints were gone.

Still, there was quite a price on his head. The owner of a bordello, the notorious "lady in red," Anna Sage, set him up. She alerted the F.B.I. about his planned movements for the evening of July 27, 1934, saying he would be at a movie theater. Agents covered two possible locations and waited for the notorious criminal to exit. Eventually they spotted him at the Biograph Theater on North Lincoln Avenue, in the company of two women.

As Dillinger walked out, F.B.I. agents closed in and ordered him to put up his hands and surrender. They claimed that he reached for something so they gunned him down, shooting him in the back. He ended up with four wounds, including the one that killed him: a bullet had entered his neck, traveled upward, and exited his right eye.

People stepped forward to collect souvenirs. Women dipped handkerchiefs in Dillinger's blood.

Taken to the morgue, the body was thoroughly examined. The F.B.I. went to take fingerprints and discovered his ploy. However, the doctors hadn't done their job. Around the acid-burned area a sufficient number of ridge patterns remained to make an identification.

93

The Biograph has the reputation of being haunted. People claim to see Dillinger's ghost outside in the alley, where he was gunned down. Whenever the theater is renovated, the ghost seems to appear as a bluish figure that runs, falls, and vanishes. Blue haze, however, is not as definitive for identification as a fingerprint.

Unique Identification

In forensics, there is class evidence and unique evidence. Class evidence is generic and evidential items like carpet fibers, car paint, and dirt particles can be identified only as members of the class.

Unique evidence, which investigators prefer, can identify a distinct source. In this group are tire or shoe tread patterns that have unique marks or wear patterns. For humans, unique items of evidence are fingerprints and DNA. Handwriting, too, is considered unique. Fingerprints and handwriting have seen some overlap in the forensics and paranormal realms.

The examination of fingerprints is known more technically as dactyloscopy, which is based on the fact that the smooth, hairless surfaces of hands and soles of the feet are covered with patterns of raised friction, or papillary, ridges. Those on the pads of the fingers, thumbs, and palms form patterns so unique that they can serve for individual identification.

Present on top of these ridges are tiny pores that exude perspiration, which combines with amino acids and adheres along the ridges. Thus, fingers, thumbs or palms can leave readable impressions on specific types of surfaces.

Methods vary, and with new technology are changing, but when a suspect in a crime is brought in, his or her fingerprints are rolled in black ink to reproduce the ridge patterns. Prints from both thumbs and all eight fingers are placed on "tenprint cards." Electronic fingerprint systems that scan the fingers of a suspect and store the information digitally are now widely in use. The fingers are numbered one through ten, starting with the right thumb. The left thumb is number 6. Then they get coded, along with descriptions of any extra, missing or uniquely scarred fingers.

Those prints that have been left in ink, paint or blood at a scene are called visible or patent prints; latent prints are invisible, except with certain procedures or lighting conditions; plastic prints are those left in soft surfaces, such as warm wax. The impression might be whole or partial, but even a partial print can be sufficient to provide a lead and make a match.

The characteristics that make a fingerprint unique are called minutiae, and identification via fingerprints relies on the detection of the patterns of minutiae and a comparison of their relative positions on a reference print. Examiners compare where the ridges start and end on a finger, where they split, and where and how they join, as well as where dots and other unique structures are located.

While patterns are unique to individuals, fingerprint patterns can be divided into eight basic types via specific features. Plain arches are ridges that run across the fingertip and curve upward in the middle, while tented arches show a spike. Loops, which flow inward and then recurve in the direction of origin, have a delta-shaped divergence and are either radial (toward the thumb) or ulnar (toward little finger). Whorls are oval formations, often making a spiral or circular pattern around a central point. If a pattern contains two or more deltas, it will probably be a whorl. There are plain whorls, central pocket loop whorls, double loop whorls, and accidental (a pattern that does not conform to those already described).

Sample Fingerprint

Once the basic pattern is established, examiners can concentrate on the finer points. There are several basic ridge characteristics: the ending (dead-end with no connection), the bifurcation (forked ridge), and the island (enclosed ridges) or dot (isolated point), and these may form composites such as double bifurcations, ridge crossings, or bridges. These are used as the basis for points of comparison, and some areas of the print yield more points in a given space than others.

Identification is made when the examiner decides that the degree of similarity between two prints is sufficient to conclude that both originated with the same person. Currently in the

United States there is no established minimum of points of identification to match a print of unknown origin to a reference or suspect print.

Latent prints on surfaces at a crime scene must be made visible, and the quality of the print will depend on the type of surface material. At first, prints were developed on nonporous surfaces using a soft brush with fine, gray-black dusting powder, and this is still practiced today. It works best with fresh prints, before the oils dry. The excess powder is blown off, leaving a clear impression from the powder that adheres. The print can then be photographed, lifted with a tape, or placed onto a card. Colored powders were developed to contrast with surface colors, and some powders or dyes glow under alternative light sources. Fluorescent reagents, which react with amines from body secretions, yield fluorescent patterns, which can be useful on multi-colored surfaces.

Chemical sprays have been developed that allow technicians to lift fingerprints from surfaces as rough as bricks and rocks or as slick as vinyl. The spray contains iodine-benzoflavone or ruthenium tetroxide as alternatives to dry powders, and can treat large areas much faster than powders can. It does not replace the powder, but it expands the type and quantity of surface that can be analyzed.

Prints might also be developed with chemicals like iodine, ninhydrin, and silver nitrate. The Super Glue wand is a portable system with which to fume at the scene inside cars and against non-movable surfaces.

In 2012, scientists in China announced a quick, simple method for visualizing latent fingerprints at the scene of a crime that preserves the print. Bin Su and co-workers from Zhejiang University, Hangzhou, noticed that a compound tetraphenylethene (TPE) adhered to the greasy ridges of fingerprints. TPE is non-fluorescent in acetonitrile solution, but when light with a 365nm wavelength is shone onto the solution, the compound can lose the extra energy by rotating. However, when TPE sticks to the fingerprint, its molecules clump together (or aggregate). The aggregated molecules can no longer rotate, so instead, they release the energy as light.

Fingerprints of the Dead

Parrocchia S. Cuore di Gesu in Prati, a church in Rome, has a unique museum, "Piccolo Museo del Purgatorio," in which are displayed documents, book pages, and garments which the dead have allegedly grabbed or touched and left a visible imprint of their ghostly fingertips or hands. While no print is clear enough to make a convincing comparison, each was accompanied by a story that identified a once-living person who sought something after death. Most of these people were urging loved ones to say mass for them or make some type of reparation.

For example, one deceased woman wanted her husband to pray for her soul, and she grabbed his nightcap, leaving the image of five fingers. A priest authenticated it, saying that the burned areas had been made by the dead woman's hand. (It was 1875, before anyone had taken fingerprint techniques seriously.)

As quirky as this may seem, in fact there have been a few notable attempts to try to fingerprint the dead. In a British case in 1961, the Society for Psychical Research approached the Fingerprint Bureau to use its special powder to help them fingerprint a "nonphysical entity." They had a case in which a man had reported the appearance of phantom hands in his home. If these hands would appear and press against something on which the powder was sprinkled, investigators thought it might be possible to show proof of a haunting. Even better, they might identify the deceased.

The detectives were intrigued enough to bend protocol and bring their crime scene kit to a few séances. The fingerprint examiner reportedly saw the hands and he made several attempts to get an impression, but ultimately he failed.

Years later, an enterprising television reporter had greater success. A railroad crossing in San Antonio, Texas, featured stories about the ghosts of children pushing the cars uphill over the crossing. He knew that it was based on an optical illusion, but the reporter put talcum powder on his car just to see. He watched it roll "uphill" and then went to look. To his surprise, he later reported, he had found tiny handprints in the powder.

One ghostly handprint has attracted a lot of attention, and forensic analysis has been involved.

In the latter half of the 19th century in the area northwest of Philadelphia, coal was king and the railroads were its barons. In the town of Jim Thorpe, once known as Mauch Chunk, the English and

Welsh Protestants owned the coalmines, but it was the Irish Catholic laborers who worked them.

Anger against the mining companies inspired the formation of a secret society of violent Irishmen known as the Molly Maguires. In 1869, Frank B. Gowan became head of the Reading Railroad Company. His policy was to destroy the unions, and his only opposition was the Molly Maguires. He hired Allen Pinkerton, who gathered evidence that solved several murders in the area.

One man, under arrest, tried to save himself by squealing on others. He implicated Alexander Campbell as "the bodymaster" who had orchestrated the killing. Campbell protested that he was innocent, but he was arrested and found guilty of murder. He continued to insist on his innocence, even as they dragged him from cell #17 to the hangman's noose. Legend says that just before he was removed, he placed his right hand against the dust on the wall and stated that its mark would remain forever as proof of his innocence.

After over a century, the handprint is still visible, despite efforts to erase it. The Carbon County sheriff tore down the wall in 1930 and put up a new one, but the mysterious print re-emerged. Another sheriff claimed he'd painted it over with green latex paint, but still it resurfaced.

Enter forensics. In June 1994, a local judge asked Professor James Starrs to apply his forensic techniques to the handprint. By using oblique lighting, he saw that the paint marks led up to the edge of the handprint, and with a chemical analysis, he proved it. The townspeople had perpetrated a fraud to get tourists there to see the ghostly handprint. However, if Campbell was truly innocent and his soul continues, he might offer other means to make us take his "innocence project" seriously.

Fingerprint analysis could be helpful in identifying famous or notorious ghosts who had had their fingerprints taken during their lifetimes. Once again, however, the "loops," "whorls" and "ridges" on a ghostly hand have long ago decomposed and might not leave any trace of a print. No one has yet recorded paranormal mist leaving such detailed impressions.

One thing that paranormalists can learn—and should practice as soon as possible—is the detailed databasing of evidence that has been going on for decades by law enforcement with regard to fingerprints. A worldwide database of all paranormal findings should be established and maintained for patterns to emerge and currently collected data to be compared with past and future data.

A handprint is one type of identifier, but there are others, and forensics has developed techniques to match residual evidence with its source. Among primary pattern evidence that involves a matching procedure is handwriting.

Handwriting Analysis

During the 1800s, a popular ghost technique was to use a planchette equipped with a writing device to aid the deceased to communicate in writing. In fact, one British scientist tested a planchette "guide" by asking it what word his finger was covering from a newspaper in the room. (He had placed his hand on the paper without looking.) He was surprised that the word that slowly materialized from the planchette was the exact word he was shielding.

Along with planchette communications was automatic writing, wherein a disembodied spirit used the hand of a human host to write a message. Often, the spirits using this device merely answered questions with brief responses, but some claimed to have once been an identifiable living person. In that case, their handwriting can be compared to something they wrote while alive.

Forensic handwriting analysis came of age during the trial of Bruno Hauptmann in 1934, with the acquisition of numerous cryptic ransom notes to Charles Lindbergh, the father of a kidnapped and murdered child. Although most people in a culture are taught the same basic handwriting technique, as they age they develop unique idiosyncrasies and handwriting experts are able to match handwriting to specific people. In addition, content analysis, which can identify the sources of a person's education and reading material, assists in making such an identification.

Most people learn to write by imitating a certain style, usually the Palmer or Zaner-Blosser method, but eventually idiosyncrasies develop in the way letters are formed that come from factors like education, artistic ability, physiological development, and preference. This is what makes handwriting distinct and personal. Repeated usage over a long period of time crystallizes a specific style that will show only slight variation, if any, over the years.

Both Paragraphs Were Written by the Same Person.
The Second Paragraph is the Sample of Automatic Writing

Handwriting experts study the variations in writing samples to try to determine if the same person wrote two (or more) different documents and thereby to identify the known author of one sample with the known author of a similar one. The same odd characteristics—ways of spelling a word, the particular slant or spacing, or manner of forming certain letters—are expected to show up across samples by the same person, and they're evident even when the person might be trying to conceal his or her identity.

Analysts look at the following features: class characteristics, formed from the writing system learned, and individual characteristics, or features that are not common to any group.

It is the latter that play the most important part in forensic investigation. A known specimen written by an identified person is called the "standard" or "exemplar," and it should be as similar as possible to the questioned writing, specifically containing similar words or letter combinations. The primary factors for analysis are divided into four categories:

1. Form—refers to the elements that comprise the shape of the letters, proportion, slant, angles, lines, retracing, connections,

and curves.

2. Line Quality—refers to the results from the type of writing instrument used, and the pressure exerted, along with the flow and continuity of the script.

3. Arrangement—involves the spacing, alignment, formatting, and distinctive punctuation.

4. Content—this is the spelling, phrasing, punctuation, and grammar.

If writing exemplars exist from a living person, they can be compared using forensic techniques to whatever a spirit might allegedly produce. Although a medium could claim that a death event makes post-mortem handwriting different, if living and deceased exemplars were found to match, this would be a unique bit of proof.

In addition to the form of handwriting, we can also use linguistic analysis. Also called forensic stylistics or attributional analysis, linguistic analysis involves a detailed examination of the content of a questioned document to compare what was written to what a suspect reads or generally writes. The basic premise is that no two people use language in exactly the same way, similar to the idea that no two people form their letters or numbers in the same way.

Some examiners claim that the scientific analysis of a text can detect features as sharp as anything this side of fingerprints and DNA. The pattern of unique differences in each person's use of language, along with repetition of those traits throughout his or her writing, provide the internal evidence that links a person to the questioned writing.

When examining a questioned sample, such as a letter, examiners might search text databases that could contain similar language habits. The language used by an unknown author can help establish the writer's age, gender, ethnicity, level of education, professional training, and ideology. The key items are vocabulary, spelling, grammar, syntax, and punctuation habits. Other kinds of textual evidence may include borrowed or influential source material, document formatting, and the physical document itself.

For example, if we were to examine the communications from the spirit of George Pelham (see earlier chapter), we could compare the things he discusses, and the ways he discusses them, to examples of his narratives when he was alive. If this spirit is Pelham, there should be considerable overlap in the unique aspects of the content.

As yet, no one in the paranormal world has undertaken such a comparative examination with comprehensive record-keeping.

Content known only to the ghostly writer is valuable as identifying evidence; linguistic analysis may also be helpful in identifying a particular dead person since particular speech patterns can be associated in ethnic or cultural patterns. Specific handwriting analysis could be tricky. Mark has seen psychics channel deceased individuals through automatic writing. The handwriting of the channeler changed completely, sometimes displaying a remarkable difference by wandering all over the page in unsophisticated scrawls. Comparing that to the dead person's handwriting might be helpful in solidifying an identification, but for now, the dead person's identity must already be known to secure handwriting samples.

Ghost DNA?

The analysis of the properties and effects of serums—blood, semen, saliva, sweat, and even fecal matter—is called serology. Biological evidence is often found after crimes of violence. It might be fresh liquid, coagulated, dried, or in the form of spatters, a small drop or a stain. Each form dictates a different method of preservation and collection.

We have about ten pints of blood in our bodies. When wounded, the heart's pumping action makes bodies leak or spray blood, and the behavior of blood in flight tends to be unaffected by such things as temperature, humidity, or atmospheric pressure. It remains uniform.

Despite how well the crime scene may get cleaned up, even the finest trace of blood can often be detected. Perpetrators may scrub down the obvious places, but they can still miss between floorboards, under pipes, and inside drains.

One of the earliest ways to link a suspect to the victim was through the analysis of blood types. Although Type A at the scene does not prove that a suspect with Type A blood committed the crime, it is the case that if the suspect is Type O, then he or she can be eliminated. Once blood types were isolated, other discriminating factors emerged, but none was as valuable as DNA analysis. We'll get to that soon.

If it's suspected that blood was on a surface, the first test involves moving a powerful light, such as a laser, across it. This can yield possible traces for visual inspection. If nothing is seen, a chemical reagent called luminol can be sprayed across the scene because it reacts to blood. It can reveal traces with a light-producing reaction between its chemicals and hemoglobin, an oxygen-carrying protein in the blood. The molecules break down and the atoms rearrange to form different molecules. The original molecules have more energy than the resulting ones, so they shed visible light photons. This chemiluminescence is the same phenomenon that makes fireflies glow.

The luminol procedure requires that the room be considerably darkened (which makes it great for ghost hunting), and the intensity of the glow increases proportionately to the amount of blood present. It works even with old blood or diluted stains, and can illuminate any smear marks where blood has been wiped away.

A newer technique is the fluorescein reagent. It works like luminol, although it uses two successive coatings of different solutions. It's illuminated with a UV light, and since it persists much longer than luminol, it's better for getting photographs.

DNA, or deoxyribonucleic acid, is the genetic blueprint that gives us our distinguishing characteristics. It's found in the nucleus of the cell. The DNA molecule resembles a twisted ladder, called a double helix. Although some parts of our DNA are universally human—two arms, ten fingers, two legs, etc.—certain sections contain the codes that give us our individual uniqueness. Thus, by looking at the unique DNA parts—called polymorphisms—experts can determine whether a particular strand of DNA found in a specimen is "indistinguishable from" the DNA of a particular person.

DNA exists only in cells that contain nuclei, so it's not in red blood cells, the hair shaft, or the outer layer of the skin, but is found in cells mixed in body fluids, hair follicles, tooth pulp, bone marrow, and all muscle and organ tissue.

When the DNA profile is developed in a forensic context, it's compared with a suspect or entered into the convicted offender index of CODIS. If there's no match, the profile is searched in the forensic or crime science index. If two crimes are linked, the law enforcement agencies in both jurisdictions are notified.

We have heard of no situation to date wherein paranormalists have managed to get residue from a ghost that would offer an opportunity for DNA analysis, but we did have a non-forensic incident that was suggestive.

This occurred in Gettysburg at the Daniel Lady Farm, the site of a Civil War battle in July 1863, and the place where a hospital was once set up for Confederate officers. The Gettysburg Battlefield Preservation Association (GBPA) believes that in a field across from the main house and barn the remains of soldiers may have been left behind. In 1873, eight bodies were exhumed from the field to be sent to cemeteries in the South. An exhumation team conducted an archaeological dig to look for bones and battle artifacts. Although a human collarbone was found near where the hospital was set up, no skeletons were unearthed.

Wounded officers had been taken inside the house and laid on the wooden floor. A cadaver dog brought in had signaled at a few key areas in the front room, and Luminol indicated that blood molecules were still detectable in what appeared as dark stains in the wood. Yet not long before, blood had mysteriously appeared there on the floor, photos were snapped and video of the scene was created. A sample was taken and stored.

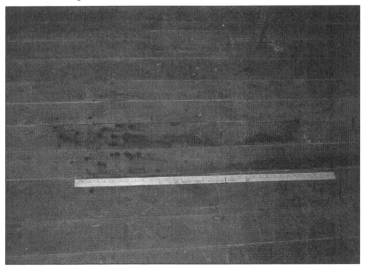

Blood Which Appeared on the Floor at the Daniel Lady Farm

Within a few hours the blood had disappeared. More photos were taken and a new video showed that an ultra-thin layer of dust had accumulated where the blood once lay. The event was similar to a "time slip" since, logically, there should have been no dust.

The sample that had been removed from the scene was still intact. It was sent to a forensic lab where it was confirmed as human. Later, a video camera with infrared lighting captured pale whitish objects rising from that area. Specifically from those spots.

As mentioned before, what paranormal investigators have yet to do is place their evidence in one large database. One can only guess at the reasons why it hasn't happened. Some involved in the field believe they are going to make a million dollars with their one piece of evidence; others are planning their own Reality TV show (which will probably never see the light of day) and so hide their evidence away. The field needs people more interested in the knowledge gained by sharing and peer review; then they need a central repository, complete with accessible computer databases. Only when that happens, as it has in forensics for decades, will patterns begin to emerge and individual pieces of data will be able to be analyzed.

Channels

Lauren noticed the security light come on outside the home she shared with Adriane Insogna and Leslie Ann Mazzara. Despite her dog's warning growl she dismissed it. She heard other noises, but she thought that one of her two housemates had invited a boyfriend in. They'd all given out Halloween candy that evening and had gone to bed around 10:30, Lauren to her first-floor bedroom at the back of the Napa Valley tract house, and the other two upstairs.

Awakened at 2:00 A.M. by the sound of breaking glass, Lauren heard a struggle upstairs. She jumped out of bed and stood in the doorway of her room to listen. A voice called out from upstairs.

"Please God, help me! Somebody help me!" It was Adriane.

Lauren then heard someone heavy-footed rush down the stairway and all she could think to do was escape out the back door, but she found herself trapped in a fenced backyard. There she hid, listening, as the intruder jumped out the kitchen window in the front of the house and ran.

Adriane cried again for help, so Lauren went back inside and dialed 911. However, the cordless phone failed to work, and upstairs she found her housemates in a single room, lying facedown and barely clinging to life. The floor was a bloody mess and Adriane was behind her bed, bleeding badly and no longer able to speak. Leslie lay in a pile of clothing, unconscious, with wounds all over her upper body.

Lauren realized she could not save them, and afraid the intruder might return, she left again, getting into her car and using her cell phone to call 911. A police officer patrolling nearby arrived at the scene, but the girls were dead.

The officer realized the killer had forced open the kitchen window to enter and had then climbed the stairs and attacked the girls. He fled the home by the same route, breaking the window's glass and leaving behind his own blood. This would provide DNA.

A task force was quickly formed. More than twenty officers moved through the neighborhood, looking for anyone suspicious, but found no one to question or arrest. They also found no murder weapon.

News of the crime in the papers the following day, November 1, 2004, stunned area residents. The F.B.I. was asked for help and within a few days community leaders offered $100,000 for information leading to a conviction. What no one knew was that the man they sought was mingling among them, consoling the victims' friends and relatives, and attending candlelight memorials. No one suspected him.

Because neither girl had known enemies and there were no obvious leads, investigators had to focus on who the victims were to try to understand how they had drawn the attention of their killer.

With this approach, once information is collected, the detectives map out a timeline to acquire a sense of the victim's movements up until the point of the crime. This may involve the day before or perhaps even several weeks before. She might have met her killer at a public place where they were seen together, or she might have purchased something where he worked. Perhaps he was a former boyfriend who'd been stalking her.

To get a sense of the possibilities, detectives question witnesses and acquaintances. Diaries, letters, phone messages, emails, or any other communications may help, especially if the victim was apprehensive about someone or had just made a new acquaintance.

Leslie, winner of the Miss Williamston beauty pageant in South Carolina, had been raised by a single mother on a farm with her two older half-brothers. She aspired to be many things, but she was drawn to the wine country. When her mother moved to Berkley, Leslie was hired as a concierge and sales rep at Francis Ford Coppola's wine estate. At the time of her murder, Leslie was dating two men, and had seen many others. People described her as a "heartbreaker," and a number of men had bought her extravagant gifts.

Adriane, local to the area, was outgoing and athletic. She worked as a civil engineer at the Napa Sanitation District. Among the plans in her immediate future was to visit her sister in Australia. She had a boyfriend with whom she had a strained relationship, so he was the number one on the suspect list. However, his DNA was not a match.

As police processed the crime scene and reconstructed what had happened, it seemed evident that Leslie had been stabbed first. They hypothesized that she was the likely target, with Adriane just in the wrong place at the wrong time. All reconstructions are based on probability analysis, which involves figuring out perpetrator and victim movements from physical evidence coupled with the most likely scenario.

Although Lauren grew terrified for her safety when the killer was not apprehended, she realized that, as the only witness, she had a responsibility to her former housemates. She agreed to go on the television program, *America's Most Wanted*, to talk about her terrible experience. She also agreed to speak with a team of psychics.

Three weeks after the double homicide, a friend of Lauren's contacted Michael Parry, a British medium now in California. His wife Marti channeled images from her husband's visions into art.

Michael went into a trance and claimed to see two girls trying to get his attention, although only one spoke to him. She said they had been murdered and mentioned the name "Lily." Michael sensed that she had been stabbed, especially in the neck. He also knew that the first officer at the scene, a female, had been unable to stomach what she'd seen. Only the investigating officers, who later confirmed it, knew this detail.

Marti offered a sketch of a white male sporting a goatee. She gave this to the investigators, and it went into the file as a potential lead. The Parrys also went to the house, which had been cleaned up, with Detective Kirk Premo.

Michael correctly identified three places where police had found the killer's blood. He also sensed where the bodies had lain. In the house, he saw images of the victim's again and Adriane conveyed to him that Leslie had been stabbed first. She also indicated that the killer was someone they knew.

About the name "Lily," Lauren could only think of Lily Prudhomme, who'd been Adriane's best friend. They had often gone places together and had even planned a vacation to Australia. Lily was now married to a man named Eric Copple, who'd done some work on the house.

DNA evidence from blood found at the scene indicated that the perpetrator was a male Caucasian and cigarette butts picked up outside had come from Camel Turkish Gold cigarettes, a brand only recently released. Since it was distinctive, it would be easier to use to confirm a suspect whenever the police developed one. In addition, the DNA from the intruder's blood matched DNA from saliva on the cigarette butts.

Over the course of a year, investigators conducted over 1,300 interviews of people who had known the victims, as well as of residents from the area. They collected 218 voluntary biological samples for DNA analysis from men who'd had contact in some manner with the victims. Detective Premo was about to contact Copple when Premo was reassigned to another investigative area. He left a file with instructions to follow up, but no one did.

Nearly a year after the incident, police released the fact that the killer was probably a chain-smoker who had stood outside the house awaiting his opportunity. They revealed the brand of the cigarettes, thinking that someone would know a person who smoked it. Lauren recalled that Eric Copple, the husband of Adriane's best friend, Lily, was a smoker. She called the police to tell them.

They placed calls to him and his wife, but none was returned. A month went by, and they still had not spoken with him or collected his DNA. Finally, in September on a Tuesday night, Eric Copple, 26, arrived at the police station. He spoke with detectives for five hours. They charged him with two counts of felony murder, with special circumstances that made him eligible for the death penalty.

Premo saw a picture of him and realized that he had a goatee, just like in the Parry's drawing. Copple had also once worked at a Napa-based engineering firm that included among its clients the Napa Sanitation District, where Adriane had been employed for three years. He'd left a year before the murders, but he had retained an association with Adriane because of her close friendship with his then-fiancée, Lily.

Apparently, he thought that Adriane was trying to persuade Lily not to marry him, so he'd gotten drunk that Halloween night and killed her. Leslie had simply been in the way. (So, in this case, probability analysis had been wrong.) Copple recalled smoking a cigarette near the garage, where a security light came on, and then used the knife to pry open a window.

He entered, climbed the stairs to the room where he knew Adriane slept, and lay down in a pile of clothing. Adriane woke up and turned on the light, startling him, so he jumped onto the bed. He thought she or someone hit him in the face, and he blacked out. He heard a sound from the other bedroom, so he went in there. He claimed to detectives that he had his eyes closed and did not recall anything that happened after that, except that he'd ditched the knife and then burned his clothing in his own backyard.

On December 6, 2006, Eric Copple pleaded guilty to killing Leslie Ann Mazzara and Adriane Insogna. In exchange, he received a sentence of life in prison without the possibility of parole.

Although the mediums' involvement in this case had not led to an arrest, it did provide information that could have been a productive lead had police been open to such information. The sketch did resemble Copple. If the reconstruction had considered Adriane as the primary victim, this lead might have been taken more seriously.

Psychic Imprints

One theory as to why a specific site might be haunted involves the "imprint" of subtle energies upon the environment. William James surmised that the energy that an individual's life generated creates a cosmic record that burns an impression into a place. This energy might be left on objects the person had handled while alive or the home in which he or she had lived. It would also cling to places where strong emotion had occurred, such as the terror that violence inspires.

During the early 1800s, a Boston geologist decided to test his wife, who claimed to have some psychic ability. He wrapped different types of rock in paper and had people who claimed to be sensitive say what was concealed. A lump of lava drew forth the response that an "ocean of fire" was pouring forth. A piece from a glacier elicited the comment, "I am frozen in it." However, there were plenty of critics of the experiment, and rightly so. The controls were lacking.

Granite is infused with quartz, which paranormalists consider the "master crystal" for conducting spiritual energy. Some scientists have proven that, under extreme duress such as torture or painful wounding, the human body produces flashes of electromagnetic energy. When porous human bones break, (as in a gunshot wound) they give off a piezoelectrical impulse, a burst of electromagnetic energy. Paranormalists believe that where violence has occurred, quartz in the ground retains this subtle energy.

Quartz at Gettysburg, Pennsylvania, site of a significant Civil War battle, is virtually everywhere—in the granite bedrock just a few feet below the soil, in the ubiquitous rock walls, in the foundations of the homes, even in the locally manufactured brick—leading to one theory about why the place is so rife with spirits: the ground absorbed a massive amount of human surprise, anger, and agony.

Under the right conditions, this theory states, this energy is released, producing a type of haunting called "residual," which acts like a looping DVD or videotape. The ghosts are unaware of the observer's presence and merely reenact their role over and over again throughout the ages. In some cases this occurs on a specific anniversary, possibly attributed to the overload of energy from living visitors to the site. An example is a "phantom battalion" seen numerous times in Gettysburg, marching through the fields, maneuvering as if preparing to meet the enemy, then vanishing. Ghost hunters are on the verge of discovering what it takes to get the environment to "replay" an historic event—create the "transducer" needed to recreate history—or, in the case of forensics, the crime.

There are plenty of tales about haunted murder items and this technology might reach the stage where it could be applied to such objects—bricks from Lizzie Borden's house, for example, Ted Bundy's Volkswagen, or the bullet-riddled bricks from the warehouse where the St. Valentine's Day massacre took place. (In fact, some collectors of these bricks claim they come with a curse. One man who had four went through four divorces, four surgeries, and developed four intestinal polyps.)

Mediums and psychics appear to be sensitive to extra-physical sources of energy. Paranormal perception, also known by some who link it with the heightened intuition used by law enforcement as "the blue sense," is explained as energy that sensitive people are able to tap into. Collectively known as *Psi* abilities, this type of perception can take a number of forms, but those that are most relevant to crime investigation include:

- Automatic Writing—using unconscious muscular energies in the arm and hand, the person allows the spirit of someone to communicate via writing. A pencil is held over paper and the deceased is invited to give a statement. It is also considered a way for a person's unconscious to communicate with his or her conscious mind. The pencil is directed by some energy other than the hand holding it.
- Automatic drawing—a similar principle to automatic writing but using art as a medium, such as in the case described above.
- "Bird-dogging"—Psychic Renie Wiley claims to place her mind

into the mind of a criminal to learn about what that person did, following the crime's trail like a bird dog. A psychic, Robert James Lees, did something similar in the Jack the Ripper case, following the trail straight to a suspect's house.)

- Channeling—allowing spiritual entities to use one's body and mind as a link between this plane and where the spirit resides, for the purpose of receiving information.
- Chiromancy—the ability to read a person's personality and future from his or her palm.
- Clair senses—any or all types of psychic sensitivity corresponding to the five senses: clairvoyance (inner sight), clairaudience (inner ear), clairsentience (a feeling in the body), clairscent (a smell) and clairsavorance (taste).
- Clair-empathy—to psychically appreciate the emotional experience or aura of a person, place or animal. A sad spirit can bring such sensitives to tears.
- Dowsing—the skill of divining for underground sources of water, items, objects or answers by means of a divining rod or an item such as the pendulum, or even by deviceless techniques. Often the pendulum's direction of swing when held on a string would determine a 'yes' or 'no' answer to a question, or locate something on a map. This is also used outside to locate unmarked graves.
- Dreams and Visions—a few days before his death, President Abraham Lincoln dreamed that his body lay in state, brought down by an assassin's bullet. Mark Twain also had a prescient dream about his brother's death three days before it occurred, right down to the white roses placed on the brother's chest as he lay in a casket. Many psychics rely on dreams to provide messages of both the present and the future.
- ESP—Extra Sensory Perception, as coined by J.B. Rhine of Duke University; it means that one can experience a thought and/or feeling from one mind to another over a distance, without physical means.
- Premonitions—in 1993, a boy recorded a description of being hit by a car and dying. Not long after, a woman ran a red light and hit him while he was walking. The manner in which he'd described his injuries matched what had happened to him.
- Precognition—seeing things before they happen, like Twain's eerie dream.

- Psychometry—using an item that had been owned by a person about whom information is sought, on the idea that energies left behind by the person inhabit things and can offer clues.
- Remote Viewing—seeing things happening in places too far from the seer for him or her to be physically seeing them.
- Retrocognition—a power that 1960s-era psychic Peter Hurkos claimed to use, wherein he would meet someone for the first time and "see" backwards to the past events of that person's life.
- Tarot Card Readings—Tarot is a deck of seventy-eight picture cards used in divination and some psychics use them to channel a reading of psychic energies along a certain track.

Some people who claim to have this perception say that it's based on the natural sense of intuition, or the way we focus our inner awareness to provide self-guidance. Others suggest that all past information resides in a field—the Akashic Records—accessible by those who can tune into it. The brain, to them, is not so much a library of past facts as a radio to be tuned into a segment of the Akashic Field. Operating beyond our conscious awareness, Psi is a gut feeling on which one acts in faith, on the border somewhere between cognitive and emotive skills. Something inside tells you, without you having to slow down and analyze it, that what you're doing is correct. Those who regularly follow this sense of direction generally strengthen its power of insight. For some people, it becomes a sort of "knowing," an inner assurance.

Intuition can take many forms:

- A feeling that something is going to happen;
- An inner voice directing us;
- The sense that we must pay attention right now;
- Any kind of fleeting sense or sudden energy;
- Any seemingly significant encounter;
- A sudden flow of inspiration;
- The easy visualization of steps in a plan;
- Finishing someone else's thought;
- Sensing a distant event that proves to have taken place;
- Getting the flash of a name and then having that person contact you.

Nearly all high profile "ghost hunters," as seen on cable TV programs, search out ghosts using instruments such as EMF meters, near-infrared video cameras and audio recording devices. While these techniques are fine, they can be supplemented with some age-old methods that almost anyone can develop. Mark calls it "Intuition Forward": developing and utilizing one's feelings about a situation to fine-tune an investigation.

Dowsing rods and pendulums—which many believe are merely gauges for the handler's psychic intuition—can be used to narrow down the field of spirits wanting to talk. For example, a spirit can be directed to swing a pendulum in a circle for "yes" or back and forth for "no." The handler asks if the spirit's last name begins with a letter from A to M. If the answer is yes, the field is narrowed further. Once the first letter of a name is found, then the second is sought using the vowels one by one. Very quickly a name can be found, then other instruments, such as recorders, can be used to question the entity.

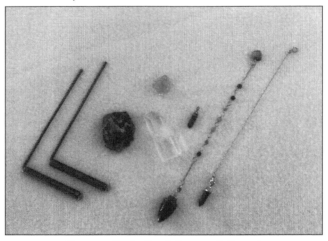

Dowsing Rods, Pendulums and Crystals

Some first-timers have done remarkably well—better than some "pros"—at remote viewing, sketching everything from the location of the doors on the side of a barn to underground water sources—all before having visited the place.

Whether this is the way that mediums and psychics connect to otherworldly knowledge is not completely clear, but in the next two chapters, we'll explore more examples of how psychics and law enforcement have worked together.

Police Psychics

George Dekle, the prosecutor for the final murder that Ted Bundy committed in 1978, published *The Last Murder* in 2012. This victim was Kimberly Leach, a 12-year-old girl who disappeared from the grounds of her school in the middle of the day. A witness saw a man leading her toward a white van. However, the search for leads proved arduous.

Ted Bundy

Although the start of Theodore Robert Bundy's criminal career is unclear, he came to the attention of law enforcement as "Ted" in 1974. Several young women had been assaulted or had disappeared in Oregon and Washington State, and when two suddenly vanished on the same day from Lake Sammamish State Park near Seattle, witnesses described seeing these girls with a slender man named Ted, who drove a tan or gold Volkswagen Beetle. He'd used a ruse to get them to accompany him.

But Bundy had moved on to Utah. As he roamed around Utah and Colorado, several more corpses of missing young women turned up. When he posed as an undercover cop to try to abduct Carol DaRonch on November 8, 1974, she fought him off and escaped.

The following August, Bundy was arrested on suspicion of burglary and DaRonch identified him as her assailant. He got jail time but escaped and ended up in Tallahassee, Florida. On January 15, 1978, Bundy entered the Chi Omega sorority house at Florida State University, raping, strangling, or clubbing four girls in their beds. Two died. He got away.

A month later, he stole a van and drove into Lake City, Florida. Here he abducted Kimberly. He raped and killed her, and dumped her body outside town. Bundy was soon arrested for driving a stolen vehicle, and was identified as the escaped killer, wanted for murder in several western states. He refused to supply any information

115

about the missing Kimberly Leach. What follows is the reconstruction effort, which included a psychic's participation.

The investigators in Lake City pieced together a scenario that linked Kimberly to Ted Bundy. They knew that he'd stolen a university van and driven to Lake City. Using the van's mileage, they narrowed down the possible area, and based on sand from the van's carpet, they pinpointed a specific area. However, this still left a lot of ground to cover.

Several psychics stepped forward to offered their impressions. In fact, certain officers were assigned to the "psychic patrol," to deal with these messages to see if any was helpful. One psychic was allowed into Kim's bedroom alone with a tape recorder, but her trance produced only static. Another psychic used playing cards, without success. (In fact, a test showed this man to be inaccurate with his divination about 90% of the time, yet he still presented himself as psychic.)

A woman from Orlando, Anne Gehman, had a reputation for finding lost articles. She responded to the task force's request that she try to get a vision about where Kimberly might be. Some of the things she said could have come from news reports, although Gehman claimed to not follow the news. (There was evidence that she subscribed to a clipping service, so this marred her credibility.)

Kim was dead, she reportedly said, and the killer's name was Ed or Ted, with the last name of Brady or Bradley. He'd been driving a van, and the investigators should track stolen credit card receipts.

Gehman also drew a map that showed two bodies of water connected to a canal. South of this area was a railroad track and a highway. North were horses and west was a picnic and camping area. Along the east was a burnt patch. In the middle, between the bodies of water, Gehman had placed an 'X'. That was for the location of Kimberly's body.

However, an aerial search showed many areas that resembled this crude map—too many to effectively search. The detectives were back on square one, discouraged and exhausted.

The best evidence they had was soil from the stolen van, which a geologist had identified as being from the Suwannee River area. In fact, a mounted search team had already tried going through this area, but a rainstorm had driven them out. As another search was launched, Dekle came along.

He describes how they were driving near a sinkhole and found a dirt road that led them to a burnt field. They turned around and saw a large sinkhole filled with water. They got out to look and discovered a canal connecting one water-filled sinkhole to another. It was just like Gehman's map, although she had pinpointed an area about twenty miles away.

"To the south, we had US 90 running parallel to a railroad track. To the east we had a burnt field. To the west was the Suwanee River State Park. Although we didn't verify it we decided that the park would naturally have picnic tables and campsites."

But what about the horses?

One member of the team knew of a man who lived to the north of the sinkhole who had horses on his farm. This revelation gave everyone a chill.

Dekle didn't know it, but at that moment, he was within ten yards of Kimberly's body.

They decided to search the area the following day. Within a few hours, they located Kimberly Leach's mummified remains—"almost exactly where Gehman had marked her X." Bundy had stuffed her beneath a deteriorating hog pen.

No news clipping service could have given Gehman such a distinct image. Dekle does say that if they'd never spoken to Gehman, they would eventually have found the body on the strength of the geologist's report. However, noticing a sinkhole area that resembled her drawing in such detail made them focus on that area right away.

Bundy was eventually convicted of this murder, receiving a death sentence. (Reportedly, his ghost now visits mediums, trying to help with unsolved murders to gain redemption.)

Working With Law Enforcement

Despite the fact that skeptics galore decry the use of psychics for anything but entertainment, some officers will call on certain psychics when all else fails. The first official use of "psychic sight" during a trance in a criminal case was in 1845, when a clairvoyant fingered a juvenile suspect, who subsequently confessed. The details of the case aren't documented well enough to decide whether the psychic was just making a good guess, or perhaps knew the boy, or whether she actually "saw" the crime with her sixth sense.

In 1888, psychics got involved to some degree in the case known as the Whitechapel murders, or the crimes of the offender known as Jack the Ripper. In the space of ten weeks, from the end of August into November, someone killed five prostitutes (two of them on a single night), slitting their throats and removing pieces of some of them to carry off. The murders stopped as quickly as they had begun, and Jack's identity was never conclusively resolved. There were a handful of suspects at the time, but no one was ever charged or convicted of these brutal crimes.

To try to discover the killer's identity or when he might strike again, spiritualists all over England held sittings, the details of which were sometimes revealed to the press. From his scars to his residence to his accomplices, spiritualists provided what information they could about the killer from their impressions. One man (Robert James Lees) said that he was wearing a tweed suit, and he took the police to the home of a prominent doctor, who was subsequently hospitalized for mental illness. However, no psychic provided information that solved the crimes.

Over a century later, Pamela Ball tried to contact the victims or the killer through channeling, in which a living person becomes a means through which the dead can speak. Calling her method "evidential mediumship," she used several different means, including astrological charts of the victims, to contact someone with "inside" knowledge.

Ball received feelings such as nausea and resignation, and images of several different men, which indicated that there might have been more than one killer. She tried contacting various suspects and came to the conclusion that there were political secrets that most of the victims knew, and that's why they had been killed. She asked the otherworldly forces if Jack's identity would ever be known and received the answer, "No." She tended to support the popular idea that a member of the royal family was involved, a sexy theory but not tenable.

Although contacting victims long after a crime has occurred can be a fascinating exercise, those psychics who actually get involved in an investigation provide a better means for verification (or not) of their talents. For example, 20-year-old Stephanie Stroh went missing while she hitchhiked across the county in 1987. Her parents reported this to the police: where she'd been when she had last called home—Winnemucca, Nevada. The F.B.I. entered the case to assist. A search team drove into the Nevada desert and fliers were posted in every truck stop from Winnemucca to Reno. The police knew how easy it would be for a killer to hide a body in that vast expanse of no-man's-land.

The Strohs hired a psychic, who told them that Stephanie was dead. Her body had been thrown into a hole—a well or mine. It was near an eastern Nevada town that had four syllables in its name. There would be a strip mining operation in the vicinity, as well as a ravine and a white building. The psychic also envisioned her feet inside concrete.

The police decided to follow up on these leads, finding an abandoned road house near strip mining. There was an old dry well, which they searched. But they did not find a body. The case went cold.

Years later, serial killer Tommy Lynn Sells, who knew nothing about the psychic's vision, confessed to killing Stephanie. He claimed that he picked her up near Winnemucca and told her that he would take her to Reno. He said that they dropped LSD together, and then he strangled her, put her body in concrete, and dumped it in a hot spring. He could not recall exactly where, but his description, independent of the psychic, verifies several of the details she offered.

Tommy Lynn Sells

Detective's Test

We mentioned in an earlier chapter the advice that former New York City Homicide Detective Vernon J. Geberth offered for working with psychics in *Practical Homicide Investigation.* Geberth admits that it's controversial to work with psychics, and that police officers are naturally skeptical of their claims, but he presents the results of his research on several psychics, including Noreen Renier. He believes that if the technique has proven successful at all, it should be considered again. Yet showing no basis in science, Geberth states that psychics have learned to "control a portion of the brain which is not generally used."

While Noreen Renier apparently prefers to hold an object that had belonged to a victim at the time of the murder, and Geberth does not raise any objections, in fact such handling could contaminate evidence and make chain-of-custody claims difficult later in court. Geberth says that an earring from a victim was sent to Renier and she used it to determine through psychometry what the victim looked like and how she was killed. She "saw" tattoos on the murderer's arms and later said that her visions helped the police to track him down. Geberth notes that they arrested the guy based on physical evidence at the scene, but he leaves the impression that the psychic helped to solve the case.

Jumping In

On April 9, 2005, the *Appalachian News-Express* reported that a psychic actually found a body. Lynn Ann Maker, a "psychic detective" and "psychometrist" from Iowa, was contacted by the family of Greg Wallace, 30, who'd gone missing while driving to his job on March 14. His car had been found abandoned, with the keys inside and the hood raised.

Maker went to the site at her own expense. She held a shirt that had belonged to the missing man and sensed that he was dead and submerged. She "felt the need" to wade into a pond near the car, where police had already searched and found nothing. After taking a few steps into the water, a body floated to the surface. She recognized the deceased from photos and called 911. The Georgia Bureau of Identification said that her "find" was a coincidence.

Maker indicated that she did not know how Wallace had died and did not present herself as able to see everything. That's a common misperception, she indicated. She just takes whatever she gets. "It comes to me and I relay it," she told reporters. "God led me there."

Other psychics have made similar comments, and one person who says she possesses such second sight (and did not wish to be named) offered a description of it:

"From what I've experienced the images are quite often too fleeting. Sometimes I will get an image that is strong and sometimes only a hint of what happened. It's like when you first walk into a building with an unusual smell and as your body becomes attuned to the smell you can no longer smell it. It requires walking away, then coming back to revive the senses. I find this is the same with me when I get to an area where the senses start to work over something that happened... I have to let go and try again sometimes. It's not always the case that a person gets anything, either, if the aura energy left over isn't strong enough.

"For instance, a person may be rendered unconscious before the stabbing and cutting began, therefore lessening the impact of what the aura energy could have told a person. The greater the fear and pain experienced while conscious, the greater the amounts of aura energy left behind. If a [psychic] person was to stand or sit on the spot where someone was actually murdered, they might see some fleeting images of faces but more likely the battle itself. When one knows they are dying, they are more intent on the survival aspect and not the person's face who is killing them. Or if a body part is severed or cut, the psychic may experience the sensation of the object that penetrated them and see the loss of the limb."

Remote Viewing

Many mediums are adept at remote viewing—visualizing a scene far removed from them in distance and time. In other words they can see into the past, to scenes of a crime. During the Cold War era, both the Soviet Union and the U. S. trained gifted individuals to successfully remote view each other's secret facilities. Significant funding supported the effort. "Officially" the programs were shut down some years ago, but some former participants, according to David Morehouse in his book *Psychic Warrior*, think this is misinformation and believe that the programs continue underground.

These former remote viewers are still alive, writing books. Their stories, and the military records they reveal, are remarkable. Some ghost hunters have used the technique of remote viewing as well.

Remote viewing, strange as it may seem, works. Mark and his wife Carol were supposed to meet investigative medium Laine Crosby at Chatham Manor in Fredericksburg, Virginia, on the night their famous ghost, the "Woman in White" walks. Laine, at the last minute, couldn't make it.

Mark was attempting to gather EVP, but was getting "skunked"—having no luck at all. Carol suggested he give Laine a call and have her remote view the place. Mark called and Laine, who had never been to Chatham, said, "See the two trees up by the house?"

Sure enough, there were twin trees just outside of a room that had been used for surgery on soldiers wounded in the Battle of Fredericksburg in the Civil War.

"Go stand between the trees," Laine continued. "You'll get EVP there." Mark walked to the house, placed himself between the trees and began to get EVP.

Not only did Laine accurately remote view the trees, but she also mentioned that the "Woman in White" was standing on the balcony over the door. Obviously, she was way off on this one, since there was no balcony over the front door. But then Carol walked over to a Civil War-era photo of the house and saw that, during a past era, there had been a balcony over the door. In fact, discoloration of the brick on the building showed where it had once stood. Laine was correct, after all.

Chatham Manor

During one of the "Spirit Quest" weekends—special weekends where people stay overnight and accompany Mark's team on as many as four paranormal investigations—the participants were challenged to remote view the next investigation venue. They had not been told where they would be going, yet two sisters drew a nearly exact view from the front porch of the house toward the

122

barn. One drawing included a door on the second floor of the barn from which hay was tossed and had no steps leading to it. They even included the pond and underground feeders to the pond, later confirmed by the owner.

It's Not Always Easy

In 1980, Etta Smith, a shipping clerk in Los Angeles, heard an announcement on the radio about a house-to-house search for Melanie Uribe, a nurse who was missing from her neighborhood. Smith had an impression that the woman was not inside a building, but outside in a specific area. Although she'd never before had such an overwhelming sense of something, it was so vivid that she reported it to the police.

"It was like someone was talking to me," she said.

She believed that the nurse had been hit on the head and dumped in a canyon, which she showed to a detective on a map. She said there was a dirt path going right to her. When he seemed not to take her seriously, she decided to go have a look on her own.

As Etta drove through the target area in Lopez Canyon, she had a feeling of "urgency." Spotting some tire tracks in the dirt, she felt them and sensed the trauma that had taken place there. "It was like a thermometer going up," she later reported. She got back into her car and drove, but her daughter told her to stop because she'd seen something—a pair of white nurse's shoes.

Smith knew who was there. She drove away, and when she saw a policeman, she waved him over and told him about the body. He told her to go home. She did, but then two detectives came to bring her in for questioning.

Smith agreed to take a lie detector test, and the police later said that she'd been judged "deceptive," so she was treated as a murder suspect, strip-searched, and put into a cell for three days. Suspecting that her information about the body had come from neighborhood gossip, the police planted an undercover cop in the cell with her to try to find out why she had come forward. The cop reported that her motive was money.

But then, three men confessed to killing the nurse, and Etta was released. She says she never had another such vision. At least, if she did, she was smart to enough to keep it to herself.

Psychics and Crime - Another Side

Gift or Exploitation?

Some supposed psychics exploit gullibility and wishful thinking. For example, Gerard Croiset used psychometry and psychic impressions to find missing people and assist in criminal cases. For over forty years, he amassed quite an impressive record, until it was shown that many of his "hits" had come from published accounts in newspapers.

Dutch psychic Peter Hurkos insinuated himself into high profile cases, so that his name would be attached. He appears to have had an uncanny gift, but he wasn't as good as he (or others) claimed.

In 1941, when Hurkos lived in the Netherlands, he fell off a ladder in the Netherlands while painting a house, surviving a four-story plunge. He hit his head on the ground and, according to him, he suddenly experienced psychic powers. He was 30, and he soon started a lucrative career in the supernatural.

Sponsored by a research society, Hurkos visited the United States in 1956 and became a celebrity, offering psychic readings to Hollywood stars. Among his accomplishments by 1969, he listed his success in solving 27 murders in 17 countries. However, his findings didn't always converge with the evidence. He always insisted that he was right, even if a perpetrator was someone other than the person he'd identified.

One of his high profile cases involved the series of crimes attributed to a serial killer dubbed the Boston Strangler. Between June 14, 1962, and January 4, 1964, thirteen single women in the Boston area were victims of either a single serial killer or possibly several killers. At least eleven of these murders were thought to be victims of a single person, with two added later. Within ten weeks, in 1962, six elderly women were killed, the first four within twenty-seven days. A second wave began in December, which involved several younger women, but during the spring of 1963, there were two more older women.

All but one were murdered in their apartments, had been sexually molested, and were strangled with articles of clothing. With no signs of forced entry, the women apparently knew their assailant(s) or, at least, voluntarily let him (them) in their homes or failed to lock their doors. Most had led quiet, modest lives, although one was involved in sexual research.

Hurkos identified a suspect—a door-to-door shoe salesman with a history of mental illness. Hurkos chased around the city, trying to prove that this man was the killer and ultimately confronting him. However, the police had already investigated and cleared him. Hurkos maintained that he had the right man. Even after Albert DeSalvo confessed, Hurkos insisted that DeSalvo was lying.

Then in 1969, Hurkos was asked to consult on another series of crimes, this time in Ann Arbor, Michigan. Seven young women had been abducted and killed near the campuses of Eastern Michigan University and the University of Michigan. The killer appeared to be eluding the police. Fear had turned to panic in the community, so a citizens group called the Psychedelic Rangers hired Hurkos.

His method was to hold pictures of the murder scenes in closed envelopes, reciting reconstructions of the murders in remarkable detail. Several officers commented later that he had turned them into believers, particularly one who was accurately told that he had a gas leak in his camper.

Several times, Hurkos insisted he could solve the case within the next day or two, only to recant. He gave them a name, but it was just one more suspect to investigate. He said the killer was a genius. He also called him a sick homosexual, transvestite, member of a blood cult, daytime salesman, and someone who hung around garbage dumps. He said the killer was about five-feet-seven, blond and baby-faced, 25–26 years old, and about 136–146 pounds. Hurkos added that the killer drove a motorbike and went to school at night. He predicted that the murder count would reach 19.

On July 27, Hurkos went on television and stated that an arrest was imminent. He hoped the killer was listening, because he was going to describe him. But now he had a different set of characteristics: the killer was six feet tall and had dark brown hair. (One account holds that a girl came to Hurkos's hotel, and in the presence of three police officers, said her boyfriend fit the description. His name was John Collins, he had brown hair, was six feet tall, and rode a motorcycle.)

Then another young woman, Karen Sue Beineman, disappeared and this put pressure on Hurkos to deliver. However, a photo of her gave off no vibrations, although he believed that something bad had happened to her. He predicted that her body would be found near a roadway named Riverview or River Drive. In fact it was found several days later in a ditch alongside Huron River Drive.

Upon hearing of the body's discovery, Hurkos hit his face and said, "Her face was beat, beat, beat. It was wrinkled, like a monkey face." (However, the known victims had been beaten, too.) He described the disposal site accurately, but still could not name the killer. When taken to the site, he didn't experience his usual "vibrations," but said the man he "saw" was not an American and that he was associated in some way with a ladder.

The day after the body's discovery, Hurkos left the city, vowing to return a week later to wrap up the investigation. Before he did, John Collins was arrested. Ultimately he was convicted of the murder of Karen Sue Beineman, whom he had picked up on his motorcycle.

Hurkos had offered nothing that assisted, took credit for what others had done to facilitate the arrest, and even gave leads that went nowhere, but he did assist a Some supposed psychics exploit gullibility and wishful thinking. For example, Gerard Croiset used psychometry and psychic impressions to find missing people and assist in criminal cases. For over forty years, he amassed quite an impressive record, until it was shown that many of his "hits" had come from published accounts in newspapers.

The Skeptics

There are several famous skeptics and psychic investigators looking for fraud, such as the James "the Amazing" Randi, as well as watchdog groups around the country, who criticize and debunk psychics and channelers. Their challenges and negative evaluations tend to take the following forms:

- Psychics merely make good guesses that anyone could make, given the information in the newspapers or police reports. About a case in which a psychic found a missing man trapped in his truck in a quarry, Dr. Gary Posner of the Tampa Bay Skeptics said that, given a day or two of studying newspapers, maps and the missing man's habits, he could have come up with the same clues.

- Psychics never predict the future in a way that might stop a crime or tragic event from happening.

- Psychics only give vague information, like "old house," "bridge," or "water." After a crime is solved, it's easy for the investigators to interpret crime scenes in ways that associate with the psychic impressions, but skeptics claim the police stretch the facts to validate their use of the psychics.

When Mary Cowset disappeared from Missouri in the company of her boyfriend, Stanley Holiday, her family feared the worst. Holiday was arrested in New Jersey and he called his sister and told her he'd killed Mary, stabbing her ten times and dumping her in the weeds in Illinois. Police needed a body, but he wouldn't reveal the information, so they turned to a psychic, Greta Alexander.

She said that a body had been dumped where there was a dog barking. The letter "s" would play an important role and there was hair separated from the body. She asked to see a palm print of the suspect, so the detective brought one. She said that a man with a bad hand would find the body.

Then searchers did find a headless corpse, with the head and a wig nearby. The man who found it had a deformed left hand. Yet skeptic Ward Lucas claimed that Alexander's hints had not helped the investigation. The "s" had too many potential interpretations to have been useful. She had seen a bridge, and the river had many bridges, so that was an easy guess. Knowing the victim had been missing for months outside, it was also easy to say that the head and hair would be separated from the body.

Lucas claimed that Alexander had nothing to do with where the search was set up, yet the police say they would not have persisted in looking for so long if she hadn't insisted and would not have found the body in time to prosecute her killer.

Joe Nickell, a confirmed skeptic, set up an interesting project. He assigned twelve psychic investigators (who ranged from journalists to professors) to each study one famous psychic for a year. They were to find a single case in which the psychic actually found a missing person or solved a crime. The results showed that psychics failed to come through on scientific tests, and that, when put into such test conditions, their powers "invariably desert them." No one solved a crime during this year.

The Director of Behavioral Services for the Los Angeles Police Department devised a controlled experiment that involved a dozen psychics looking at evidence from four crimes. At the end, he stated that the psychics had scored no better than chance.

When critics claimed the sample had not been representative, the study was undertaken once again, with two control groups added: college students and homicide detectives. The psychics produced more information, but the students had a better overall accuracy rate. No group produced significant information that would have been useful in solving the crimes.

What do skeptics have to say about the apparent successes of some psychics who work with the police?

- Some famous cases could not be verified and checked.
- The psychics used ordinary means of obtaining knowledge about a crime.
- The police later remembered what the psychic said as being more specific than it actually was.
- Vague generalities can be made to fit almost anything.

In some cases, such as the following two, psychic involvement has actually made a situation much worse.

The Mystery of Nell Cropsey

Late in 1901, 19-year-old Nell Cropsey disappeared. She had lived with her family in a riverside home in Elizabeth City, North Carolina. Her boyfriend, Jim Wilcox, was the chief suspect, since he was the last to see her. Five years older than Nell, Jim was the son of the county's sheriff. He claimed later that he'd left her on the front porch of her house after he'd spoken with her briefly about a "serious matter," and then went home.

Nell's sister, Ollie, who knew that these two sweethearts had soured on each other months before, had seen Nell go out to the porch just after eleven o'clock the previous evening to talk to Jim. She hadn't come back in.

Later that night, as the family searched in vain for the missing Nell, her father went over to the Wilcox house. Jim said he'd broken up with Nell. The next day, Jim was arrested for kidnapping and the suspicion of murder. Under interrogation, he gave several stories, including that Nell had mentioned suicide and that she'd suddenly stopped acting like his girlfriend.

When bloodhounds turned up nothing, the family despaired. Then a spiritualist from Norfolk, Virginia, named Madame Snell Newman, said that Jim had killed Nell and thrown her into a deep well near an old house. Madame Newman mentioned several more accurate details, and said there had been an accomplice.

A citizens' committee brought Madame Newman to town and took her out to the countryside. Like a bloodhound on a scent, she led a rather large pack of people for miles, down one trail after another. They found two wells, both of which held only water.

Two days after Christmas, a pair of fisherman found Nell floating in the river. An autopsy showed that she had not drowned, and a bruise on her forehead indicated foul play. Jim was arrested, tried and convicted for it. Sent to prison, he was pardoned after fifteen years, but later in life, a despondent drunk who couldn't find work, he used a shotgun to blow off his head.

No physical evidence tied Jim Wilcox to Nell Cropsey's death.

Visions and Confessions

Three teenagers, a boy and two girls, were found stabbed to death in Speegleville Park near Waco, Texas. It was July 13, 1982, and though there had been plenty of violent incidents that year, this one was different. It wasn't an obvious drug deal or a domestic dispute, nor an incident due to stress brought on by the stifling heat.

Among the three victims, the medical examiner counted forty-eight stab wounds. Kenneth Franks had twenty, ten of them into the heart, but several had clearly inflicted great pain before he died. Jill Montgomery had taken seventeen wounds, mostly to the chest, and her throat was cut. There were also small bruise marks on the right shoulder and chest, and the girl had been stripped and sexually violated. Raylene Rice was stabbed nine times, with evidence of genital injury.

Carlton Stowers describes the incident and investigation in *Careless Whispers: The Lake Waco Murders*, including the psychics who "saw" the killers in visions.

As the murder was occurring, Karen Hufstetler living near Dallas, Texas, had a nightmarish vision of two men brutally killing three teenagers and transporting their bodies. She had fallen asleep after work in front of the television, and upon awakening, she was startled by a vivid image of a car moving slowly through an unfamiliar wooded landscape. She made out three males inside, and two females. A bearded driver and an Indian-looking man were clearly older and the other three were teenagers.

This was nothing new to her. Karen had experienced such visions since she was a child. As this one continued, she saw an earlier moment where the three teenagers were together at a picnic table. The brunette appeared to like the boy and Karen sensed that one of the three rings on her fingers had come from him. Then the two other men drove up and the boy introduced the bearded man to the girls. They all got into the car and at some point, the Indian man reached over the blond girl in the back seat and stabbed the boy with a knife.

The car continued and then pulled over. The driver got out, removed the boy's body and left it off the road. The brunette got out and ran, but the driver caught her and forced her to watch the other man put a knife into the throat of her friend. She broke away and ran again, but was caught and brutally beaten before she was finally murdered.

The man took one of the rings off her finger and put it into his pocket. He then carried her back to where the other bodies were, stabbed her again several times, took a lock of her hair, and left the scene of carnage. He and the other man drove to where they had found the kids and the driver tossed something into the lake that, when it hit something, had a metallic sound.

Karen did not know who any of these people were, and found nothing about such an incident in the Dallas paper the next day, so she had no idea what to do with these horrifying images.

That same night, Glenda Thomas had a similar experience. She was resting from studying for a nursing exam when the vision hit her. She described two men similar to what Karen Hufstetler had seen, but thought there was a third one in the background. They had not known the victims and had faked a need for assistance. Taking the teenagers with them in a red van, they had killed them near a road. On the arm of the leader was the tattoo of an eagle.

Glenda had then tried contacting the victims through automatic writing and said she had heard from Raylene, who had indicated that a bra was around her leg—an accurate and specific detail not reported in the papers. Raylene also said that she had not known the killers. Glenda sensed something about a ring, but did not know what it meant.

In the meantime, the police were losing ground as several days passed with no clear leads. They decided to bring in John Catchings, a psychic who claimed a 60% success rate. After spending time at the scene, he said there had been three men involved and one of them had murdered the kids in a flat-bottom boat. He believed that a dark-haired woman in her twenties would offer important information.

In fact, the detectives had their eye on a 19-year-old brunette. Her boyfriend, David Spence, was in prison for another crime. He was acquainted with Muneer Deeb, who had reportedly confessed to a friend of the victims' that he had killed them. But he'd passed a polygraph and was allowed to leave. Yet he'd told someone else that he'd taken out an insurance policy on a girl, Gayle Kelley, who closely resembled one of the victims.

Detective Truman Simons, to whom Glenda Thomas related her vision, surmised that Deeb had hired Spence to murder Gayle, and Spence had made a mistaken identity, killing Jill and her friends. Deeb had expected to collect on an insurance policy that he'd tricked Gayle into signing. Shortly after the murders, Spence had been arrested for aggravated sexual assault. There he'd talked far too much, claiming to be the kids' killer. Eventually he'd been tried and convicted, along with two accomplices. Deeb, too, was convicted, and he and Spence got the death penalty.

David Spence

Both were then granted second trials. While Spence was convicted a second time, again receiving the death penalty, Deeb was acquitted in 1993. He insisted that neither he nor Spence had been involved.

So, how did the psychics stack up? Glenda Thomas had been correct that Spence had wings tattooed on his arm. Both she and Karen Hufstetler (who eventually went to the crime scene and declared erroneously that victims were killed where they were found) had seen the ring that Spence had taken from Jill as a trophy, but contrary to what Catchings had said, the brunette never did provide information. Nor was there a flat-bottom boat.

The only aspect of the psychic testimony that had actually been instrumental in moving the case along was an item from Glenda's vision that Truman Simons had used to get a confession from one of the accomplices. Recalling what Glenda had said, Simons described to the man what he'd been wearing that night at the crime scene, leading him to believe the police knew more than they actually did, so he admitted to the crime. Yet he lied in several places.

Unfortunately, this story has been regarded as one of those successfully solved by psychics, when a look at the investigation shows that this clearly is not so. Not only that, considerable doubt about Spence's guilt has clouded the case.

Many of the homicide investigators involved believed that Spence had been pressured into a false confession. Two jailhouse snitches recanted their original testimony, saying they had been bribed to make statements against Spence. In addition, Spence's post-conviction lawyers from the Texas Resource Center organized a blind study in which five odontologists said the bite marks that helped to convict Spence could not be matched to Spence's teeth.

Although there had been a great deal of contact between the victims and the killers, there was no physical evidence other than the bite mark connecting the crime to Spence or his co-defendants. Strands of hair, including pubic hairs that most likely came from the killers, were found on the victims, but an F.B.I. analysis determined that none came from Spence or his supposed accomplices. The car that Spence had supposedly used to transport the victims had not even belonged to him at the time of the triple homicide, and no forensic evidence was found in the car he did own.

Many people believed that Texas killed an innocent man. While two women unattached to the case clearly received visions that seemed linked—and even assisted in the interrogations, no physical evidence ever corroborated it. And while nothing fully exonerated Spence, there was clearly reasonable doubt.

This case provides a powerful illustration of why investigators should be cautious about psychic visions.

Murder Mystery

A strange tale unfolds around a key figure in the paranormal field, D. Scott Rogo. There's quite a bit of misinformation about him, often to enhance the role that psychics played in helping to solve the mystery of who had murdered him in August 1990. In fact, the case remains unsolved, which makes it a good example of the kind of case we think would effectively showcase what a P.F.I. team could do.

Biographers have helped to establish the facts, which are as follows.

Born in 1950, Rogo had an out-of-body experience when he was just 11 years old. He published his first articles while still a teenager and his first of thirty books when he was 19. Rogo was interested in many "fringe" subjects, including reincarnation, ghosts, poltergeists, UFOs, and ESP. As a respected researcher, he made regular contributions to such magazines as *Fate* and *Psychic*. Not only did he explore these subjects as thoroughly as he could, but he also exposed frauds. Quiet and unassuming, he had many friends among writers and psychics. He lived alone in a nice area of the San Fernando Valley, the upscale Northridge.

Reporter Michael Connelly covered the story for the *Los Angeles Times*. A neighbor of Rogo's had noticed the sprinklers running for two days in a row at his home. Rogo was frugal and the LA area was under a water restriction due to a drought, so the neighbor thought it was odd that Rogo would waste so much water. He notified the police.

Around 1:00 in the afternoon of August 16, an officer went to the 18100 block of Schoenborn Street. He turned off the sprinkler and tried to get someone respond to his knock. The place was quiet. The officer noticed a side door standing ajar, so he entered.

He walked around until he saw a body on the floor of the den, lying in a pool of blood. The officer called it in.

Just 40 years old, Rogo had been stabbed to death. There was no sign of a break-in or a struggle, so investigators surmised that he had known his assailant. People who knew Rogo were aware of how often he helped strangers who were down on their luck. He might have picked the wrong person to help.

Rogo's parents were able to describe pawnable items that were missing from the otherwise orderly rooms, and Rogo's wallet was empty. He carried little cash, but he always had some. No one had gone through his valuable books or paged through the manuscripts in his home office. He lived a low-key life and had no financial issues.

An investigation ensued, but it quickly ran aground. When found, Rogo had been dead at least 12 hours, possibly as long as two days. The last time he was known to be alive was on August 14. He'd spoken to his publisher and volunteered that day at an AIDS hotline. On Tuesday evening and Wednesday afternoon, a bartender at the In Touch bar had seen Rogo with a man. However, people who knew Rogo said that he wouldn't have left his sprinklers running for 24 hours, so the Wednesday sighting seems unlikely.

Friends of Rogo's invited psychics to weigh in, and one was Armand Marcotte. He did several readings. He handled books that Rogo had treasured, as well as Rogo's letter opener. He said that the perpetrator was familiar to Rogo, and was young and Hispanic. His name was Al or Albert and he wore a uniform for work. The crime had been spontaneous and passionate, escalating from an argument over a small sum of money.

Other psychics had overlapping results, but the written accounts show only the points in common, not the points of divergence. One person said that three men had been involved, but one had left before the murder. Most agreed that two men had killed Rogo.

The police eventually arrested friend of Rogo's, John Battista, a 29-year-old Hispanic man. He went to trial, and after a mistrial, he was convicted in 1992 of second-degree murder. However, in 1996, due to prosecutorial misconduct, the conviction was overturned. A bloody fingerprint on a glass in Rogo's home, along with prints on the wall, did not match Battista, although the police are convinced that he was inside Rogo's home during the murder, possibly holding him while another man stabbed him to death. Battista would not admit to anything or name an accomplice.

In *The Psychic and the Detective* (1995), author Ann Druffel gives Armand Marcotte credit for helping to solve the Rogo murder, although he clearly did not. She states that he "saw" a fingerprint on a glass that would match the killer and erroneously says it matched Battista. She also writes that numerous psychics agreed that the other man involved would be caught.

Nothing like this has yet occurred. Marcotte says that Rogo came to him as a spirit and gave him information about the other man, as well as stating that a third man had been present. Yet the police could not make these leads pay off. Thus, the case remains open for analysis.

Perhaps Rogo was just a generous guy, as many stated, or perhaps he was giving help to young men as part of an arrangement. He was gay, so it's most likely that his arrangements were related to sexual partners. If there was an argument, it might have been about blackmail or about a payment or price the killer believed was unfair. In such a case, Rogo would have invited the man (or men) inside, but an argument could have set off a fight that was over as quickly as it began. The stabbing indicates anger more than a means to achieve a robbery. In fact, the DA had stated that it was one of the most vicious he'd ever come across.

A behavioral profile would take a full accounting of victimology. That Rogo was gay and was known to pick up men "down on their luck" would be a significant factor. So might his reputed frugality and his fame, such as it was. His assailant might have spotted him as an easy mark, as well as a man with wealth (a common misperception about authors). If he could not get what he hoped, he might have stabbed Rogo in frustration.

However, the vehemence of the assault suggests an emotional involvement, possibly anger over a misunderstanding or a refusal to do something that the assailant expected. The robbery appears to be more of an afterthought. This looks more like a crime arising from a relationship of some type than an attempt to commit a planned robbery. This would be especially true if there was only one weapon but two assailants. However, we did not have access to the autopsy report.

Despite the psychic impressions, nothing indicates that more than one man was necessarily involved. If Rogo did indeed return from the dead to avenge his murder and bring the perpetrators to justice (and one wonders why he didn't place a few postmortem calls, as he had documented in his book, *Phone Calls from the Dead*), why didn't he keep visiting one of these psychics until the murder was solved? Why did he offer such vague information about the accomplice? Why did he allow three men into his home, two of whom he did not know?

What appears to be most annoying to police officers is that when crimes happen—especially high profile crimes—psychics (sometimes hundreds of them) call in offering information. Regardless of whether the information is even acknowledged, the psychic then goes on to claim that the police consulted with him or her on that case. This appears to have been the MO of more than a few famous psychics, whose "cases" reportedly numbered into the hundreds. When they lie or exaggerate, they lose credibility, for themselves, and for psychics in general.

Putting It All Together

Katherine had the chance to work on the following case with former F.B.I. profiler John Douglas, because even after a century, it remains a controversial case. In many ways, it was the O. J. Simpson case of its time. Katherine not only studied it as a crime reconstruction with one of the world's noted experts but also undertook a paranormal investigation. The following is from her point of view.

On August 4, 1892, Andrew Borden, age 70, and his wife Abby, age 65, were murdered in their home in the port town of Fall River, Massachusetts. Andrew's corpse was discovered in a semi-reclining position on the living-room couch, his battered head resting on his rolled-up coat and his face cut open. There were blood spatters on the floor around him, up the wall, and on the picture hanging over the sofa, but oddly, Borden's clothing was undisturbed.

It appeared as though he was napping, except one eye, sliced in half, was staring at the ceiling. His head was bent slightly to the right, and eleven fierce blows had cut into his face, severing his nose. It appeared that someone standing over him had attacked him from above.

Body of Andrew Borden

But it was the middle of the morning on a summer day. Andrew usually locked the door when he came home. At that time, he was unaware that his wife, Abby, lay dead in the guest room upstairs. Had he merely climbed three or four steps to see over the landing, he could not have missed her battered corpse. But apparently, he had rolled his coat into a pillow—an act quite uncharacteristic of him—so he could take a mid-morning nap. He never woke up.

It was Borden's adult daughter, Lizzie, who found him. She was thirty-two and, as a single woman, was living at home. The only other person in the house that morning was the live-in maid, Bridget Sullivan. A cousin, John Morse, had come to visit and was staying in the guestroom, but he'd gone away to see friends that day. So, it was Lizzie who came into the living room and found her father lying in a bloody mess.

Lizzie Borden

She wasted no time. Lizzie called up to the third floor where Bridgett was resting and sent her right out for the doctor. She told Bridget that someone had killed her father.

A neighbor, Mrs. Churchill, arrived and asked Lizzie where her mother was (Abby Borden was actually her stepmother). Lizzie told her that Abby had gone out that morning, but then added that she thought she'd heard her return. Mrs. Churchill said they should search the house and Lizzie asked her to do it. Lizzie remained in the kitchen at the back of the house while Mrs. Churchill approached the stairs.

As she reached the second-floor landing, she looked to her left and noticed a dark object on the floor on the far side of the guest room bed. She squinted, saw clothing, and realized that it was another body. Mrs. Churchill rushed down the steps, told Lizzie, and ran for help.

The police arrived and discovered that Abby Borden, lying facedown, had been hit multiple times with a sharp weapon, possibly a hatchet. Her blood was dark and congealed, and it soon became clear that she'd been killed some time before Andrew. This meant that the murderer had been lurking in the house all this time, near Lizzie and Bridget.

Yet there was no evidence that he'd tracked blood from one room to the next, or had washed himself in the guestroom basin, or hidden in the single narrow closet upstairs. The place was too small for him to have successfully escaped detection. There was no blood on the stairs or into the neighboring bedrooms.

As investigators questioned Lizzie and Bridget, they learned that it was the family practice to keep all doors on the first floor locked. Yet on this day, Lizzie claimed to have been in the barn, leaving the back screen door unlocked. She was in the loft for twenty minutes, she said, although investigators found no evidence that the thick dust on the floor had been disturbed. In addition, no footprints were evident around the house and as investigators fanned out they learned that no neighbor had seen strangers in the Borden yard. The identity of the culprit remained a mystery.

Theories about who did the ghastly deed ranged from sister Emma, who was visiting friends in another town; Bridget, who had been told to wash windows when she was feeling ill; John Morse, the brother of Andrew's first wife, who had unexpectedly arrived the night before; Andrew's supposed illegitimate son, who lived in New York; a wandering maniac with an ax; and, of course, Lizzie.

She was arrested and her contradictory answers at an inquest, coupled with a friend's grand jury testimony that she had burned a dress, resulted in a trial for murder. Among other evidence against her was the fact that she had tried purchasing poison the day before and no evidence corroborated her statements.

There was talk that Andrew Borden had decided to draft a will, which would have given his estate to Abby and her family rather than Lizzie and Emma. In addition, a hatchet turned up in the house that seemed to match the cuts in both skulls. Lizzie had also burned a dress.

Yet Lizzie hired a crack defense team and the men of the jury were reluctant to find her guilty of a capital crime. Notable evidence was ignored, such as a spot of blood on one of Lizzie's dresses. The jury acquitted her.

Within six months, Lizzie had sold the murder house at 92 Second Street with most of the furnishings, using her considerable inheritance to purchase a mansion in the wealthy area of town—to where she had begged her father to move for years. When she died, she was buried in the family plot with her murdered parents and her sister, Emma, from whom she'd become estranged.

Borden House

Through the years the murder house became a rooming house, bookie joint, and Kewpie doll factory. Then, in 1947, John and Josephine McGinn purchased it for their printing business, signing the sales agreement on their wedding anniversary, August 4—also the anniversary of the murders. (In fact, Mr. McGinn died a few years later on July 19, Lizzie's birthday.) When their granddaughter Martha inherited it, she and her partner turned it into a bed-and-breakfast. (They sold the business a few years later.)

My Investigation

I had heard that one could now book a room in this place, and I was determined to do so, for two reasons. I was the researcher on this case for John Douglas, so I thought I would bring along my ghost hunting equipment as well. I'd already met Mark Nesbitt in Gettysburg while learning about the technology involved in ghost investigations, so between these two endeavors, I prepared to think along parallel lines: the forensic investigation and the paranormal one. I booked the guest room where Abby had been whacked nineteen times.

When I arrived in Fall River, I stopped at the local museum where many of the crime scene objects and photos were on display. I read through several documents and made notes, especially regarding the environmental forensics (weather reports from that day and the house's location in comparison to the rest of the town). Then I visited Oak Grove Cemetery to see the Borden family plot.

I was aware from newspaper accounts that a law professor, James Starrs, had recently visited to attempt to exhume Andrew and Abby's skulls. On the day of their funeral in 1892, the burial had been halted. There at the gravesite, the police had informed the mourners that the pathologist wished to conduct another autopsy on the skulls, so the heads were removed and the headless bodies were buried. In a forensic lab, the heads were de-fleshed so to make plaster casts from the skulls. Reportedly, the skulls were then placed into boxes and buried in the Borden family plot.

A key part of the prosecutor's case against Lizzie was that a certain hatchet had inflicted those wounds in the skull. One of the skulls was introduced at the trial and the person who testified inserted the hatchet into the cut in the skull to show that it fit. Starrs had decided that this had been unscientific, so he hoped to perform this same act himself. If he could show it was not the murder weapon, although it would not exonerate Lizzie entirely, he thought it would demonstrate how weak the prosecution's case against her had been.

Starrs had made a mold of the suspect hatchet, still in the custody of the Fall River Historical Society, and sent it for scanning electron microscopy. He had also used ground-penetrating radar that indicated that there had been two separate burials. However, he was stymied in his attempt to exhume the heads. The descendants of the Bordens challenged him in court.

Finally, it was time for me to go see the house where the bloody double homicide had occurred. With help from crime-scene photos, the house had been designed to resemble its condition on that infamous August morning. They had duplicated the furnishings, floral wallpaper, dark woodwork, and patterned rugs of the era, right down to a replica of the sofa on which Andrew's corpse had lain. Much of the hardware, woodwork, and some of the windows are original. A display case in the dining room—furnished with Lizzie's own former table and chairs—was filled with authentic items owned by the Bordens, and guests were shown the type of kitchen stove in which Lizzie had burned the suspicious dress. (It wasn't the same one, but a replica.)

I spent the afternoon reading the investigation reports and trial records for myself. I found plenty of suspicious unexplained aspects of this crime that seemed to have been overlooked during the investigation.

For example, a bucket of bloody clothing in the basement was never fully examined. Bridget, who did the laundry, said it had not been there when she was in the basement the day before. Yet, Lizzie, who claimed it was from her menstrual cycle, said the bucket had been there for several days. At the time, males did not wish to ponder such matters (and even the all-male jury avoided the subject), so no one had bothered to see if what Lizzie had claimed was true. Right there, I knew, could be the very evidence that Lizzie had done the deed, washed herself off, and stashed the bucket in the basement. I passed this on to Douglas.

I also believed that the psychological angle on this crime contradicted the notion that Andrew Borden had rolled up his expensive coat to use as a pillow. He was a parsimonious man who always hung his coat up to make it last for years. He'd hardly have rolled it on a hot and muggy day to place under his sweaty head for a nap. So if the killer had done it, what reason would there have been?

If we consider that Lizzie did it, we can imagine the following scenario: Andrew comes home and hangs up his coat. Lizzie has already murdered Abby an hour earlier and she prepares to murder Andrew. As he lies down, she grabs his coat, pulls it over her, backwards, to protect her dress, and stands over Andrew, at his head, but partially protected behind the doorjamb that's near the couch. She brings the axe down on him nine times, quickly, then rolls the coat and places it under his head to get soaked with his blood. Free of blood spatters herself, she calls the maid to go fetch the police. (Or, perhaps she did get some blood on her face, so she washed it off and stashed these rags in a bucket in the basement while Bridget was running off the fetch the doctor.)

An analysis of how Andrew had bled into the coat after the attack could have offered something definitive, but no one thought to do it. (They were in fact doing this sort of analysis in 1892; by then, Sherlock Holmes had been in print for over a decade, pressuring law enforcement to be analytical and observant.)

In addition, Lizzie had a little problem with stealing, so we know she was no angel. She was also angry with her father for his cheap ways and had been restless to use the family money for a better life.

Oddly, Lizzie had been with her sister the day before, on her way to visit friends in another town, but she'd doubled back and stayed in a nearby boarding house for several nights before going home just before the murder. (One must wonder why?) She also attempted to purchase prussic acid in a neighborhood far from her own, and she showed no sorrow in the wake of the double homicide.

In fact, upon finding her father freshly killed, she had seemed unalarmed that the killer might still be there in the house. (Some theorists offer that Lizzie killed her father because he'd molested her, but Lizzie was quite obsessed with the family fortune. Abby, in fact, took more blows, and it was well known that Lizzie resented her and feared that she could inherit everything.)

It's possible, I thought, that Lizzie's sister, Emma, knew of the plan, because when she was summoned by telegram to return home, she did not take the first train back, or the second or even the third. She took her time returning.

Cousin John Morse, too, had behaved suspiciously. Although he was clearly away when the murders occurred (and thus had an alibi), when he saw the crowd gathered at the Borden house as he was walking back, he didn't rush as one might expect to find out what was going on. Instead, he picked up an apple and ate it, watching the activity before proceeding.

In addition, Bridget said that Andrew had brought home a parcel that morning that seemed to be a bunch of papers tied together, but it seemed to have vanished. No one knew what had been burned that morning in the grate, but the ashes resembled rolled-up papers. Also, Lizzie gave over a dress to the police that she said she'd been wearing on the morning of the murders, but Mrs. Churchill, who had seen her, insisted it was not the dress Lizzie had worn. No one could locate the one she described.

This evidence and much more implicated Lizzie, and possibly some coconspirators, but she was never convicted. No one was, and no wandering maniac was ever found. My own opinion after seeing the case details was that the forensic investigation—even for this time period—was lacking. But there was more. I also noticed that after the murders, there had been a paranormal investigation.

Before retiring, I sat on the Victorian sofa that stood in the spot where Andrew had been whacked and read through some notes about what a pre-trial session with an Ouija board had once delivered. This record was actually included in the prosecutor's notes from Lizzie's trial.

According to the "spirits," Lizzie had done it and her original intent had been to poison her family with prussic acid. Lizzie had worn trousers during the killing, according to the Ouija "forces," which she then buried in the yard. She also burned the handle of the hatchet she'd used and put its head in a box in the basement. Lizzie's cousin John Morse assisted her with the cover-up, as did Emma and her personal physician. The Ouija indicated that Lizzie would never be found guilty of the crimes.

Her motive? Money. She had overheard talk of an investment that she had hoped to inherit being put instead into Abby's name.

The board got the time of the murders pretty close, too: 9:30 and 10:45. (But then, this psychic revelation occurred after these times had been estimated by the coroner and published in a newspaper.)

But were there any ghosts here? I'd heard that two psychics had insisted after reading the house's spiritual vibes that Andrew had been killed in the kitchen and dragged to the couch (forensic evidence indicates otherwise) and that a former owner's dog always refused to go up the front staircase that led to the guestroom. I knew there were other stories, but I didn't ask for the details. I wanted to keep my mind free of prejudice.

Finally, I went upstairs, to retire to the room where Abby was killed. I would be alone in the house that night, I knew, because I was the only guest. The owners did not stay.

I glanced first into Lizzie's dark room, but saw nothing unusual. Then I went into the guestroom. A greeting placed on the bed included a cute note: "If a door should open or close on its own, or a light go on or off, please take this in good humor, as we are mere mortals and cannot control our supernatural guests. They are generally well-behaved, but sometimes tend to get a bit mischievous."

I hesitated about shutting the door, but once I did I quickly locked it. When I was ready with my recoding equipment and camera, I turned off the lights and got into the antique double bed with the towering dark wood frame, lying on the side next to where Abby had fallen to the floor while blows were delivered to her skull.

I placed the voice recorder on the table next to me and pressed the button to turn it on. The red light told me it was recording. Staring at the ceiling, I listened for noises.

There was traffic outside, but inside felt like a tomb. I let my hand drop over the edge of the bed and then leaned closer to touch the spot where Abby, suffering from fatal wounds on the back of her skull, had breathed her last. But there was no cold spot. Finally I drifted off. I'm a light sleeper and I woke up a couple of times in the night to listen. Nothing.

When the sun rose and brought daylight into the room, I lay for a moment and recalled that I'd been dreaming about a young woman who'd been talking to me via the recorder. I couldn't recall the details of her face, but she'd seemed to be saying something urgent. However, to my distress, I also couldn't remember the words. I sat up and reached for the recorder, hoping it had captured something.

To my dismay, it was off. No red light.

I couldn't believe it. At some point during the night, for some reason, I'd shut it off (or someone had). It had recorded something, but only a few sounds, and they were too faint to interpret. My ghost hunt at the Lizzie Borden house, so rich with possibility the night before, had failed. Disappointed, I got dressed and went downstairs.

Martha was cooking breakfast, which came with similar fare to that which the Bordens had eaten before dying (except the meat stew), and topped off with a cookie shaped like an axe. It even had red dye along the sharp edge.

I told Martha what had happened to me and she sat down to describe the ghostly figure of an elderly woman who'd been seen by other guests in the room where I'd slept; in fact, she had gently tucked them in. There was also an old-fashioned sewing machine in the corner that reportedly had started up on its own, and a few guests had seen the impressions of heads on the pillows. Martha showed me two photos taken by guests that showed shadowy figures that looked very much like spirits.

Then one of the tour guides, Amanda, who'd had doors mysteriously lock on her while showing people around, offered to take me into the cellar, where in 1892 the police had searched for the murder weapon and found a hatchet head rubbed in ashes. (Recalling what the Ouija board had said, this was an interesting discovery.) The cellar was dusty, dark, and cool, used mostly for storage. Amanda and I walked around, keeping quiet and soaking up the eerie atmosphere. Then I turned on the recorder, let it run for a few minutes, and took a breath.

"Is there anyone here with us?" I asked.

We could barely see each other, but Amanda watched, wide-eyed, as I waited a while longer for a potential response. We heard nothing as they stood there, although I could see that the erratically blinking recorder light indicated activity. Finally I stopped it, pressed the playback button, and heard my recorded voice ask, "Is there anyone here with us?"

That was followed by a resoundingly gruff, "Yes!"

We turned and shot up the steps.

Once we were out of the cellar, we listened to it over and over. Amanda was curious now. She wanted to listen to the brief recording from the night before. I handed her the recorder and she listened intently, certain she heard a woman talking to a male.

"She is telling him not to hurt you," Amanda said. "He's talking to her, but he wants only to talk to you. She wants you to turn it off. That's what she's saying."

I hadn't told Amanda about the dream of the woman talking urgently to me.

Although my paranormal investigation of the Borden case moved me no closer to solving this still-unsolved double homicide (and it was among my earliest experiences with such an investigative approach), when I combined it with the forensic evidence, I thought some of the unanswered questions in this case had some real leads for further exploration. I was convinced that Lizzie had done the deed and the forensic evidence had been available but had been ignored.

John Douglas agreed that the evidence could have been handled better and could have been given more weight in the trial—especially the bucket of bloody rags. He also thought that the judge had been out of line instructing the jury to include Lizzie's fine character in their deliberations and to discard the entire case if they didn't agree with even one aspect of the prosecution's argument. Douglas performed a victimology from known facts and described the strategies he would use if he were to question Lizzie himself.

He believed the incident was a personal-cause homicide. Since nothing was taken from the house, this ruled out burglary. He believed the evidence pointed to a domestic incident, pre-planned. Both murders involved overkill, which indicates longstanding anger. Abby, in fact, was straddled during the attack, with the killer looking her in the eyes at times as she struggled for her life.

Douglas ruled out an intruder, because such a person would want to get in and out fast, especially during the middle of the day. This person had to have remained in place, quietly hiding in a cramped space, for over 90 minutes. And if he (or she) was intent on Andrew, and had killed Abby incidentally, why didn't he also kill Lizzie and Bridget?

Douglas also ruled out a contract killer, who would have either been more careful or would have tried to make the murders appear to be the result of a burglary. If Lizzie and Emma had hired him, he wouldn't have made the evidence point to Lizzie.

A disorganized axe maniac would probably not have been able to hide himself in this small house and remained still for the time between the homicides. He wouldn't have been in that kind of control of himself. He would have left plenty of blood evidence.

Douglas decided that, had be been consulted, he would have told local police that this had been the work of someone close to the family, with knowledge of their schedules and of the house layout. Because Emma was away, this leaves only Lizzie and Bridget. Douglas believed that Bridget had no motive and did not have the personality structure to support considering her to be a killer.

Now we're down to Lizzie. She was an unmarried spinster with little hope for a suitor, grandiose airs, and a belligerent temperament. She resented her father because he refused to use his money to keep his family in style. Although Andrew was generous to her, she was unappreciative. She was also worried that the family money could go to Abby, who had already been given some property. Lizzie viewed herself as a victim.

On the day in question, she claimed to have gone into the barn to make sinkers for fishing, but she had not been fishing in five years. She had also gone to "visit a friend" just as the rest of the family grew ill from something they ate.

Douglas saw the personality and pre-offense behaviors in Lizzie, and the crime scene indicators pointed most strongly to her. She found her father's axe-hewn body, but did not rush out to get help. She seemed unafraid to be in the house, and seemed to know that the killer was not still present. She also sent someone else looking for Abby, which is a common behavior in domestic murders.

Despite her acquittal, it seems clear from a forensic analysis that Lizzie was the killer. Perhaps a more focused paranormal investigation would shed more light.

How a Paranormal Team Would Investigate

Katherine's investigation would have benefited from another investigator or two. Protocol for "Team Nesbitt" would include a preliminary investigation, interviewing the owners and selected workers in the house, and recording their interviews. Occasionally, such as during an interview with the owner of Fall Hill, a beautifully restored (and legendarily haunted) home outside of Fredericksburg, Virginia, a disembodied voice overlays the voice of the owner to state, "Hear me out!"

For the Borden house, having a medium involved in the preliminary investigation is probably unnecessary—too much information about the murders is already out in public sources—the medium could just be remembering from his or her subconscious rather than picking up anything new.

After gathering the experiences of the individuals closely associated with the house, we would conduct a more thorough investigation, using equipment and pairing those investigators using "detecting" equipment (EMF meters, quick-read thermometers) with those using "recording equipment" (digital cameras, video recorders, digital audio recorders, or even note-takers). We'd separate into teams according to floors and begin sweeping the house.

If any "hot spots" emerge, communication would be attempted via audio recorders (for EVP), pendulums, or dowsing rods (for basic "yes/no" communication).

If the physical items from the murder are available, psychometry could be attempted for any information that technique might yield. A medium could be invited to the primary investigation to give clues to those attempting EVP as to whose spirit might be present and willing to communicate. Perhaps a computer using talk-to-type software can be set up in a closed room to see if any "automatic writing" will take place.

Day or night doesn't matter for the investigation, but relative quiet does, so a time period when there are no guests would be ideal. An infrared "Trail Cam" could be set up in a room and the room locked overnight. Any motion in the room will set it off and a photo will be exposed.

After the investigation is over, the results (photos, audio recordings, notes) can be downloaded into computers and analyzed and a report produced.

Ghostly Witnesses

The first exoneration of a wrongful conviction in the U.S. involved an alleged ghostly witness. It happened in 1812 in Manchester, Vermont, when a man named Russell Colvin disappeared. Townspeople knew that his brothers-in-law, Stephen and Jesse Boorn, disliked him, so they were suspected of doing something to him. However, no information of Colvin's whereabouts turned up, so the case went cold.

Seven years later, an uncle of the suspects complained of a recurring dream. In this dream, Russell Colvin appeared and described his own murder. His remains, he said, could be found in an old coal cellar that stood in the middle of a field on the Boorn farm, which they used to grow potatoes.

When the cellar was searched, items identified as Colvin's turned up, but no bones. However, a dog digging around a stump pulled out some bone fragments. Three doctors said they were of human origin, so Jesse was arrested.

Soon, a jailhouse snitch said that Jesse had confessed that Stephen and their father had murdered Colvin. To save himself, Jesse admitted that his brother, living at the time in another state, had killed Colvin, but Jesse denied his father's involvement. Then he recanted. Stephen returned to clear his name, but under pressure confessed to the homicide. He claimed self-defense.

The primary evidence came from witnesses who had seen the brothers arguing with Colvin on the last day he was seen. In December 1819, both Boorn brothers were convicted. Jesse received a life sentence, but Stephen was destined for hanging.

An article was published about how supernatural intervention had inspired a confession and closed the case, and two people who read it knew that Russell Colvin was still alive. His ghost couldn't have appeared to anyone. However, they could not persuade him to return to Vermont. Finally, someone tricked him into going, and when he arrived, the brothers were immediately exonerated and released.

Due to rumors that the ghostly dream had been a centerpiece of the case against the brothers (although it had not), editorials were written demanding that testimony based on supernatural forces be excluded from the courtroom.

Justice

In another case later that century, blacksmith Erasmus Shue arrived in Greenbrier County, West Virginia, from the town of White Sulphur Springs. Almost immediately after meeting him, Elva "Zona" Heaster fell in love. After a whirlwind courtship and against Elva's mother's pleading, they married in November 1896.

Zona's mother, Mary Jane, disliked the man, especially after she discovered that he had been married twice before and that one of the former wives had died under mysterious circumstances. Then Zona grew pale and taciturn, and she began to show bruises on her face and body. In early January 1897, she became ill. She soon died.

On January 22, 1897, a boy discovered Zona's lifeless body in the house she kept for Erasmus. When Dr. Knapp arrived, Erasmus was cradling his wife in his arms. Strangely, he'd placed a stiff collar around her neck and continued to cradle her head while the doctor examined her. The doctor found no pulse. One source claims that Dr. Knapp cryptically listed the official cause of death as an "everlasting faint." Another says it was heart failure—a strange cause of death for such a young woman.

During the funeral, the apparently grief-stricken husband remained at the head of the coffin, tending to the scarf wrapped around Zona's neck. He insisted it was the style she liked, although no one else remembered her ever wearing a scarf.

Shortly after the funeral, Mary Jane claimed she began receiving "signs" from her deceased daughter. First, when Mary Jane tried to return the bed sheets to Erasmus, he wanted nothing to do with them. She decided to wash them, and she reported that the water turned pink before it went clear. A pink stain remained on the sheets. Taking this as a sign from her daughter, Mary Jane prayed for divine guidance.

One night, she saw Zona standing in her bedroom, dressed in the clothes in which her body had been found. When Mary Jane tried to approach this figure, it disappeared. However, it returned the next night and revealed that Erasmus had beaten and strangled her. The apparition actually turned its entire head around to demonstrate a broken neck. It returned twice more with the same message. Mary Jane touched the figure and felt how solid it was before it disappeared.

Mary Jane approached the county prosecutor. Although skeptical of the story, he was convinced by her sincerity. He called in Dr. Knapp who admitted he had not done a thorough examination. The prosecutor ordered an exhumation and autopsy, which revealed that Zona had died from a broken neck.

Erasmus was arrested, although he insisted he was innocent.

His trial began on June 30, 1897. Defense attorneys pointed to the original death certificate's cause of death as "heart failure" and also tried to pin the blame on the boy who had discovered the body. Although Mary Jane said nothing of her daughter's ghostly visit, the defense got wind of it and used it to try to discredit her. The tactic backfired.

During her testimony, Mary Jane recounted four visits from her daughter, who'd told her that during an argument Erasmus had "squeezed her neck off at the first joint." She testified that the ghostly figure had turned its entire head around to prove the neck had been broken. When asked if she believed she'd seen her daughter's ghost, Mary Jane said she'd thought that her daughter had been present in the flesh.

Perhaps it was the fact that Mary Jane Heaster was considered a pillar of the community, a good, educated Christian woman not subject to hallucinations, that sealed Erasmus's fate. Despite a lack of physical evidence, the circumstantial evidence was strong. He was found guilty.

It's easy to dismiss this tale as something from a long past century, but more recently, testimony from a ghost was actually accepted in a Canadian court.

Lady From the Closet

Rui Marques worked as a janitorial superintendent in Yorkville, near Montreal. When a 38-year-old real estate broker, Lisa Posluns, was handcuffed, sexually assaulted and murdered on November 2, 2002, Marques was initially treated as a suspect. In fact, he had the security codes and keys to her office at 94 Cumberland, where her body was found. While he was not her killer, he ended up playing a vital part in the killer's apprehension.

Sergeant Michael Walters and his partner responded to the call from Lisa's sister that she was missing and had not been in her apartment. Lisa's office was on the fifth floor, but nothing was found there, so Walters searched the other floors. On the ground floor, he saw a pool of blood outside a utility room, along with footprints and blood smears on the wall. Walters called his partner to assist him.

They found a security guard to open the closet, at which point they determined that the lock was broken. Inside, a female lay on her left side, with a bloodstained jacket thrown over her head and shoulder. One eye was open, staring in a way that confirmed she was dead. It was Lisa. She had been stabbed seven times, and in a final indignity, her throat was slit. The officers started an investigation.

Since Marques needed access to the offices to clean, it made sense that he had a key, but that didn't help to ease suspicions. Yet finally he was cleared when his DNA was compared to the crime scene sample.

About four months later, Marques was cleaning an office at 94 Cumberland Street, the same office building where Lisa had been murdered. According to him, as he worked on putting a gleam on a black tabletop, he saw a reflection and looked up. A shadowy figure appeared in front of him. He recognized it as Lisa Posluns and watched, startled, as it pointed to the table. He later said that "the hair stood up on my arm," but the apparition faded before he could say or do anything.

Marques told no one at first, but when police eventually questioned him about some of the workers in his employ, he thought about one of them, Nelson DeJesus, who always wore black. Recalling how the apparition had point to the black tabletop, he thought he'd been offered a clue.

Marques recounted what he knew. He told investigators that DeJesus had encountered Lisa Posluns at the building on at least one occasion, had noticed her, and had even referred to her around other workers as "hot."

Then on November 5, as several cleaners entered the building after the investigation, DeJesus had volunteered a comment that he could not have killed her because on that weekend he'd been working at Mississauga's Square One shopping center. In addition,

DeJesus had once taken bags of salt from the utility room, so he knew about its existence, including that the lock was broken.

The police arrested DeJesus, based on the circumstantial evidence and his criminal history as a convicted rapist. His DNA implicated him. In addition, he'd been carrying what appeared to be a rape kit—a knife, handcuffs, and a balaclava. Charged with first-degree murder, DeJesus went to trial in February 2006.

Surprisingly, Marques's report about the ghostly visitation was allowed in court, and he described his experience before a judge. Defense attorney Mitchell Chernovsky was skeptical and asked Marques if he might have been drinking that day. He denied it.

The trial ran for several months, concluding on April 8 with a verdict. Based largely on DNA evidence from semen and saliva samples on Posluns's clothing, along with the victim's DNA on DeJesus's knife and handcuffs, the jury convicted DeJesus of the vicious sex murder. He'd served just four years on a prior rape conviction, but this time, perhaps thanks to the unquiet spirit of his victim, he was never getting out again.

The Garden City

Savannah, Georgia, was founded by James Oglethorpe in 1733, on the Savannah River in southeastern Georgia. It was America's first planned city. For a while during the 18th century, Savannah was Georgia's capital and became a shipping and cultural center for area planters, leaving it with a historic district over two-and-a-half-square miles, set up in a grid of tidy squares in which one thousand historic buildings still stand.

Among the most infamous buildings is the red brick Mercer House on Monterey Square, initially owned by Confederate General Hugh Mercer, the great-grandfather of singer, songwriter and lyricist Johnny Mercer. Built in 1861, it eventually came into the hands of Jim Williams, an antiques dealer who was responsible for saving and restoring around fifty of the town's historic buildings. Millions of readers and movie fans know Williams as the charming but slightly sinister character at the heart of John Berendt's "nonfiction novel," *Midnight in the Garden of Good and Evil*. Few know about his tremendous contribution to the city's preservation efforts.

Mercer House

Williams lived in the grand Mercer House, which he spent two years restoring and from which he ran his international business in antiques. He bore great passion for preserving Savannah's history, and he's credited with asking a priest to exorcise one of his restored homes on East St. Julian Street that had so much persistent "activity" that Williams could not get the carpenters to work on it. He himself heard footsteps and loud crashes that did not belong there.

Each year, Williams threw *the* Christmas party of the season until 1981, when he shot and killed Danny Hansford, a young man who lived with him. Claiming self-defense during an argument in which Danny approached him with a loaded gun, Williams went through three separate trials, assured by his investment in voodoo magic that ultimately he would be acquitted. And he was—at least by the jury. He threw one of his famous galas in honor of his freedom.

Some say that Williams fared poorly at the hands of Danny's ghost. He remained in the house and at the age of 59, he died of a heart attack. In the novel, the voodoo practitioner whom he had consulted had warned Williams that Danny was angry and must be appeased. Apparently, Williams failed to take this seriously.

155

People still debate over whether Williams killed Danny to shut him up or whether he truly killed in self-defense. It's difficult to tell from a "nonfiction novel" in which numerous facts have been altered, but in *After Midnight in the Garden of Good and Evil,* author Marilyn Bardsley makes a thoroughly researched case for self-defense against an out-of-control Hansford. There's little doubt that Hansford had a death wish and had asked Williams what it would take to get Williams to shoot him.

In any event, there appears to be some unsettled energy from a complicated relationship at the murder scene.

A few years after Williams's death, there were reports from people who'd come to view this infamous house on the anniversary of his annual parties. They saw lights ablaze and heard the sound of revelers, despite the fact that no one was throwing a party at the time. Others have supposedly seen Williams wandering in one of his other restored homes, so he seems to be enjoying his spectral stay on earth.

Danny was buried in section 8 of Greenwich Cemetery, next to the more famous Bonaventure Cemetery. Scenes from the book and movie indicate that his spirit remains restless. Described by one female character as "a good time not yet had by all," he was a high-maintenance hustler and alleged drug dealer and abuser who did not hesitate to make demands on Williams, his benefactor.

Katherine went to Hansford's grave and turned on a digital recorder. After she asked if anyone wanted to communicate (meaning anyone dead), she recorded a voice that clearly said, "This ain't Dee?" It almost seemed posed as a question, but upon listening to it more closely, it sounded more like an insistent claim.

We'll revisit this apparently restless entity later, when yet another incident related to Hansford's death happened.

Victim of Injustice

Gay Street is one of the oldest streets in Knoxville. From atop Gay Street Bridge, one gets a good view of the Tennessee River. One of Knoxville's ghosts used to haunt the place as well.

Local legend tells the story of a man who claimed he was wrongly convicted of murder. The actual date is difficult to find but it was while they still used lanterns to light the bridge. Many in the community believed that the man was innocent, but he was convicted anyway, and sentenced to death by hanging.

It was decided that he would be hanged from the third lantern on Gay Street Bridge, where they often executed criminals. Just before he died, he proclaimed that there would always be a sign as proof of his innocence. For years thereafter, the third light on Gay Street Bridge failed to work, and a legend grew up that an innocent man was reminding the citizens of his wrongful execution.

After the bridge was reconstructed, however, that problem was resolved.

The Boys

Young Bobby Franks, 14, willingly accepted a ride from two older boys, Nathan Leopold and Richard Loeb. It was 1924 in Chicago, and cars were exotic. Once they were away from prying eyes, they hit Bobby with a chisel, and then shoved a rag into his mouth to smother him. He died in the car's back seat.

Afterward Leopold and Loeb drove some distance away so they could strip their victim and pour acid on his face and genitals to prevent people from identifying him. Then they ate dinner with the body in the car as they waited for darkness. Finally they tossed the mutilated corpse into a culvert where Leopold often went birding, and returned home to place a call and write a ransom note for $10,000 to the boy's parents. They believed they had committed the perfect crime.

However, the perfect crime is generally never what it initially seems. The boy's body was found the next day and quickly identified as the missing Bobby Franks. Nearby in some grass, investigators found a pair of glasses, dropped there by someone. These were no ordinary spectacles. They had a set of unique hinges that were easily traced to Nathan Leopold.

The police arrested Leopold and took him in for hours of questioning. The explanation was simple, he maintained. He'd been in that area birding. Suspicion fell on Loeb as well, because the two were friends, and he was brought in, too. Yet neither broke, and there was insufficient evidence to charge them with anything. They were free to go.

Search for the Body of Bobby Franks

Leopold remained calm and quiet, feeling superior, but Loeb shot off his mouth to friends and reporters, offering theories about the murder and even suggesting that if he were a killer, Bobby Franks was the perfect victim. This brought attention back to the two men, and because the ransom note appeared to have been written by an educated person, investigators found samples of Leopold's typing. They matched.

Under interrogation again, one of them was caught in a lie, which precipitated confessions and accusations from each man that the other had committed the murder. As they provided details, the murder was revealed as a means of entertainment for two bored intellectuals.

"It was just an experiment," Leopold said. "It is as easy to justify as an entomologist in impaling a beetle on a pin." They had wanted to test their ability to plan and carry out a crime without being caught. Neither expressed remorse or thought that what they had done was reprehensible.

At trial, mental health experts tried to "explain" their degenerate behavior, but the judge was unimpressed. Yet he was also reluctant to sentence such young men to die, so after famed attorney Clarence Darrow gave a moving speech, the judge gave them life in prison.

Until 1971, the ghost of Bobby Franks was reported around his family vault in Chicago's Rose Hill Cemetery.

Loeb was fatally stabbed in prison, but Leopold was paroled after 33 years, living out the rest of his years in Puerto Rico. He died in 1971.

Famous Haunted Crime Scenes

Bonnie Parker liked to write poetry about the exploits of her lover, Clyde Barrow, although she also predicted their violent demise. Deputy Ted Hinton was one of the six officers who ambushed and shot the couple to death. He believed that Clyde brought out something in Bonnie that developed her dark side. She had plenty of chances to walk away, turn him in, and say no to the crimes they were committing, yet she stuck with him to the bitter end.

During the 1930s, when people were suffering from a nationwide Depression, outlaw gangs made headlines with their sensational bank robberies, shoot-outs, and escapes. One troublemaker in Dallas, Texas, was Clyde Barrow. His first killing was an accident, when a bullet ricocheted off a safe. He hadn't pulled the trigger, but his presence there convinced him he'd end up executed. This added an edge to his adventures: he had nothing to lose, and Bonnie apparently found this exhilarating. Together they went on a spree of robberies, and then began to kill, taking on and losing partners, and always staying together. Police chased them from state to state, but they eluded capture.

Finally, they were ambushed.

On May 23, 1934, six officers awaited the couple on a lonely stretch of road near Gibsland, Louisiana. They had gotten a tip that the couple would be coming down that road in their car. The officers settled in for a long vigil, but finally, they heard the car. When it came in sight, stopped by a man Clyde knew who faked a broken-down car, officers started shooting.

"For a fleeting instant," Hinton writes, "the car seems to melt and hang in a kind of eerie and animated suspension...Clyde's head has popped backward, his face twisted at the shock of pain as the bullets strike home."

The execution lasted about twelve seconds. The car took 167 bullets, and a coroner later counted the number of wounds that the outlaws had received. Bonnie and Clyde were each shot more than 50 times. This kind of overkill attested to the fear that somehow Clyde would manage yet again to escape.

The outlaws were towed to town in their decimated car. People came from miles around to look at them and touch the "death car." They also flocked to the place where Bonnie and Clyde had met their match, to see the blood and places where bullets had penetrated trees or ground.

Bonnie and Clyde After the Ambush

Despite Bonnie's desire to be buried next to Clyde, their respective families separated them in death. Perhaps this is why their ghosts can be seen either at the monument that was raised where they died or at the formerly lavish Baker Hotel in Mineral Wells, Texas, where they reportedly liked to go dancing.

Cold Blood

On November 15, 1959, in search of a safe inside the farmhouse in Holcomb, Kansas, owned by Herbert Clutter, Dick Hickock and Perry Smith slaughtered the family of four and then made a run for it. The newspaper story about the murders ran for just a few paragraphs, but it got the interest of writer Truman Capote.

"It suddenly struck me," he said in an interview with *The New York Times*, "that a crime, the study of such, might provide the broad scope I needed to write the kind of book I wanted to write.

Moreover, the human heart being what it is, murder was a theme not likely to darken and yellow with time." What he wanted to accomplish was nothing short of "literary photography."

So Capote packed up and went to Kansas with his friend Harper Lee, and then spent the several years of his life writing the American classic, *In Cold Blood*. Not only did he learn about who the Clutter family had been and how the townsfolk reacted to this brutal crime, but when the killers were caught, he got to know them and even attended their execution.

Hickock, a psychopathic drifter from a stable home, had met Smith in prison. Smith had bragged that he'd once murdered a man, so Hickock thought he could use Smith to pull off the murder of this rich farmer that he'd heard about from a fellow con. Herb Clutter, 48, had a safe full of money, Hickock believed, and it would be easy pickings.

Once released from prison, they went to Kansas and collected what they would need for the job.

"No witnesses," Hickock insisted.

Waiting one evening until the Clutter home looked dark, they went inside, cut the phone lines and roused Clutter out of bed. Tying up his wife and two teenage children in various rooms, they insisted he open the safe. He told them there was no safe. That's when they got upset and slaughtered everyone in the house.

Clutter Farmhouse
Photo Courtesy of Sally Keglovitz

When the Clutters missed church the next morning, friends went to find out what was wrong.

Nancy Clutter, 16, full of hope and promise, was found first. She had been shot in the back of the head at close range. She was lying on her side, facing a wall that was covered in a spray of blood. Her hands and ankles were bound, but the covers had been pulled over her, as if someone had thought to tuck her in.

Mrs. Clutter was on her bed, shot dead, with her hands tied in front of her. Her mouth had been taped with adhesive and her eyes were wide open in fear. She had probably guessed her fate.

Kenyon was lying on a basement couch, his head cradled on a pillow, but he was bound hand and foot, with tape over his mouth. He'd been shot squarely in the face, at close range.

The last body found was Herb's. He, too, had been shot in the face, but his throat had been cut as well. Tape was wound around his head and across his mouth, and his ankles were tied together. He was sprawled on a mattress box in front of the furnace. Next to him was the bloodstained imprint of a shoe or boot.

No one had any idea who could have done this. Clutter had no enemies. The family members were kind and gentle. Everyone liked them. Then investigators learned about the inmate who'd told Hickock about Herb Clutter's safe. The search was on for Smith and Hickock.

Capote saw them after their arrest and spent considerable effort getting them to talk to him. It was never quite clear which one had committed the murders. Hickock, who was the first to break down and confess, denied committing any of them, but Smith said that he'd done two and then had handed Hickock the rifle and told him to finish it. Then he'd amended his statement, because he didn't have parents and Dick did, so he didn't mind taking the full rap.

The Clutter house has changed hands several times since then, but some people say that Nancy's ghost has been seen walking the halls of her former home. Given the shocking and sudden violence there, it wouldn't be surprising.

New York Notoriety

The Morris-Jumel mansion on 175 Jumel Terrace in New York City was built by Roger Morris before the Revolutionary War, and it once served as George Washington's headquarters. Although five ghosts apparently haunt it, the one most people claim to have seen is the specter of Eliza Jumel, who inherited her husband Stephen's money after he died.

Morris-Jumel Mansion

They took over the place in 1810, but apparently all was not well, for Eliza was allegedly having an affair with former Vice President Aaron Burr. Quite mysteriously, in 1832, Stephen fell onto a pitchfork and died. Almost immediately, Eliza married Burr, but apparently, they had company. A 1916 publication indicates that there was a ghost in the house, and these rumors persisted through the years.

The Burr marriage lasted only three years before they were divorced. Eliza became reclusive, and she was a frightening sight to behold, with false teeth, unkempt hair, soiled clothing, and ungainly large feet. Finally, dementia overcame her and her babbling drove away even the staunchest relative. In 1865, she died alone in the mansion.

Within three years, people were telling stories about seeing her on the premises, clad in a white dress. This attracted paranormalists.

According to ghost investigator Hans Holzer, there was suspicion that Eliza had killed her first husband, Stephen, so Holzer took a psychic into the place. The psychic channeled Stephen's spirit and heard him say that he had indeed been murdered...and he'd been buried alive!

Many Ghosts, Many Paths

During the 19th century, when Sarah Winchester grew paranoid about the people who had been killed by her father-in-law's invention, an highly effective repeating rifle, she engaged in something quite radical.

In 1862, Sarah had married William Wirt Winchester, heir to the Winchester fortune. They had a daughter together, but soon William and the child died from illness. Sarah became reclusive and rather eccentric. Since she now managed some $20 million and owned nearly half of the profitable company, she knew the rarified world of wealthy people who, short of breaking the law, can do whatever they please.

Attempting to communicate with her deceased loved ones, Sarah turned to Spiritualism. She invited the best mediums that money could buy to conduct séances in her home. One of them, Adam Coons, told Sarah that he could "see" and "hear" William, who stated that the family was cursed and that Sarah should make amends with the victims of the Winchester rifle. Otherwise the curse would claim her as well.

William supposedly guided her to an 8-room house on 162 acres in the California's Santa Clara Valley. Growing more paranoid, Sarah hired contractors to make additions, one after another. This remodeling lasted 38 years and employed more than twenty fulltime carpenters. At times they built entirely new rooms, hallways, and staircases; at other times, they demolished their work and started over.

There was no rhyme or reason to the architecture; the place, which eventually spread over six acres, was more akin to outright chaos. There were secret passages, stairs and doorways that went nowhere, and rooms built with strange angles. Many rooms had thirteen windows with thirteen panes of glass or thirteen lights.

By the time Sarah died in 1922, at the age of 83, the massive four-story building (three stories had collapsed in the 1906 earthquake) contained 160 rooms, several towers and cupolas, numerous chimneys, three elevators, over 2,000 doors, more than 1,000 windows, two ballrooms, dozens of corridors, several upside down newel posts, and forty staircases (one of them with stairs only two inches high). In other words, it was a maze designed to confuse those spirits that might try to harm her. She also ordered a number

165

of rooms to remain unfinished in order not to anger those who wanted her to keep building.

Winchester House

In addition, she had the carpenters work on two areas specifically for the ghosts. Both were windowless rooms and one, the Blue Room, was a secret chamber. In here, at midnight every night, Sarah sat in special ceremonial robes to engage in some activity that remains unknown. She would ring a bell to let the spirits know she was there, and occasionally she would set out elaborate dinners for a dozen at a time.

In her will, Sarah asked her heirs to continue to maintain the house as a haven for spirits, but they sold it instead, and today it's a museum that hosts tours, including special Halloween treats. However, the tour is limited and many of the rooms are closed off.

Not surprisingly, psychics have been drawn to the building and some report that it's definitely haunted. A few have claimed to see Sarah Winchester herself. Visitors also hear the usual accouterment of haunted places: voices, footsteps, slamming doors (probably when the door clearly opened to a wall), and creaking stairs. The estimated final cost of the home was well over $5 million—quite a lot for those days.

Sarah Winchester

Residual Evil

In 1969, Charles Manson urged cult members to go on a killing spree. He'd formed this group from wayward kids in the Haight-Ashbury district of San Francisco, giving them a home on a ranch outside Los Angeles and a sense of belonging to something. His disciples were known as "the Family," and his vision of "Helter-Skelter" meant that blacks would rise up to massacre whites. However, they would need the help of a white tribal leader to govern things, and Manson was the man for the job.

On August 9, he sent his disciples to kill some prominent Hollywood people, telling them to make it look like the job of black militants. At a house on 10050 Cielo Drive rented by Roman Polanski, they used guns and knives to slaughter five people, including pregnant actress Sharon Tate. Then one of the killers wrote the word "Pig" in a victim's blood on a door.

The following night, they did the same to a married couple, Leno and Rosemary LaBianca. They carved "War" into the man's chest and used blood to write "Death to Pigs" and "Helter Skelter" on the walls.

Cult member Susan Atkins spilled the beans while in jail for another crime, and the killers were arrested, tried, and convicted. Manson was convicted of being the mastermind or puppeteer.

Charles Manson

Several stories arose that the ghost of Sharon Tate can be seen wandering the property, where the original house was demolished in the 1990s. Reportedly, she asks to be taken away. Someone else has seen an image of victim Jay Sebring standing in a bedroom.

Shadow Experiments

New Orleans is known for its ghost stories, and in the midst of the French Quarter is a Creole-style mansion on Royal and Governor Nicholls Streets that draws a lot of attention. It was once the home of Dr. Lalaurie and his wife Delphine.

Delphine was a reputedly beautiful woman with long, black hair, and she and her husband were renowned for throwing extravagant parties. They had many slaves and seemed a respectable pair, but little did townspeople know what Madame Lalaurie did to make her slaves submissive.

She had already been in court over charges of brutality, and on one occasion after complaints of abuse, several slaves had been removed from the home, but few people would speak out against this couple, so they were never arrested...not even after a young girl jumped to her death from the second floor to escape her harsh mistress. Then one night in 1834, a fire brought a volunteer fire brigade to the home and they discovered the Lalauries' gruesome secrets.

As the brigade doused the flames, they smelled the stench of death, so they broke into a locked attic room to find a truly disgusting scene. According to several accounts, dead slaves were chained to the walls, but those still alive were housed in cages, starved or maimed by medical experiments. One man had been surgically transformed into a woman, and a woman's arm and leg bones had been broken and reset at odd angles. Another woman's skin had been peeled off, while the lips of a third were sewn shut. A few had been dissected, with their organs still exposed. Scattered around the room were pails full of body parts, organs, and severed heads.

LaLaurie Mansion

169

A lynch mob was formed, but the Lalauries had escaped and were never heard from again. Renovations years later uncovered the skeletons of slaves apparently buried alive, but no one knows how many unfortunate victims these two brutes actually had.

This building soon developed the reputation of being haunted, and people avoided it. Although it is a beautiful residence in a desirable location, it sat vacant for forty years. Someone took a chance and purchased it, but several successive owners reported such problems that it again sat vacant for a while. Currently it is occupied.

Stories include sightings of a large male in chains, a woman who shouts in French and carries a whip, pictures inside thrown from the walls, cameras not working, and furniture that moves around on its own.

Bohemian Arena

The Hotel Chelsea is at 222 West 23rd Street in the New York City area of art galleries and flea markets known as Chelsea. This eleven-story building went up in 1884 as a residential co-op. The hotel's reputation as a "cauldron for creativity" came from the numerous artists, writers, actors, and other creative types who have stayed or lived there.

Among them were William Burroughs, Dylan Thomas, Mark Twain, Eugene O'Neill, Tennessee Williams, Bob Dylan, Thomas Wolfe, Arthur Miller, and O. Henry. Andy Warhol filmed *The Chelsea Girls* there, and several prize-winning works were penned there, including Wolfe's *You Can't Go Home Again* and Miller's *After the Fall*. One musician, Schizo, said that he'd never written before, but at the hotel, he wrote forty songs. A few writers lived here till they died, such as poet James Schuyler and composer Virgil Thomas.

One of the sad stories involves the slow suicide of Welsh poet Dylan Thomas. In 1953, he went from his rooms to the White Horse Tavern. He claimed that night to have seen the gates of hell and then proceeded to drink 17 shots of whiskey. He made his way back to his room, where he collapsed. He was taken to a hospital, but too late: He died there at the age of 39.

One of the reservation clerks mentioned that every Halloween the elevator constantly stops at the first floor. That's where the infamous room 100 was located. (The hotel has changed the room number.) On October 12, 1978, Sid Vicious, former bass player for the nihilistic London punk group, the Sex Pistols, called the police to report that someone had stabbed his girlfriend, Nancy Spurgeon. They arrived and found her covered in blood, lying beneath the bathroom sink. She had been stabbed with a hunting knife. Vicious was arrested. He was bailed out, but ended up dead shortly thereafter from a heroin overdose.

A blog called "Living with Legends" keeps track of the ghost sightings at the hotel. Among disembodied heads and hands, fuzzy male figures, and erratic electricity and plumbing might be Nancy's ghost.

Harbingers and Avengers

Dreams of Justice

Scores of stories recount someone awakened in the middle of the night by a presence at the foot of their bed. They recognize the person: it's Uncle Joe (or Aunt Jo) who lives hundreds of miles away.

"What are you doing here?" they ask.

"I just came to say good-bye," and the beloved relative vanishes. The next morning the phone rings. It is Cousin Joseph, Jr., calling to say that his father passed away in the middle of the night—at the hour when the visitation occurred.

In *After Death—What?*, forensic anthropologist Cesare Lombroso included an account of someone's paranormal dream. "Miss Loganson" was in Chicago when she dreamed of her brother, Oscar, who lived fifty miles away, being shot and killed. This dream recurred several times, so she began to think that he might be dead and his ghost was trying to tell her something. When the family learned that Oscar had disappeared, they took police to his home. He wasn't there.

But Ms. Loganson didn't stop there. She recalled details from the dream and led them to a neighbor, Mr. Bedford. When they forced open his door, they found blood in the kitchen. The girl insisted that her brother had been buried under fresh pavement. The police ordered an excavation and soon found Oscar's overcoat. Digging five feet deeper, they discovered his corpse. Bedford, who was now on the run, was arrested.

We should note that this story occurred during the 19th century, before the requirement for probable cause for search warrants. These days, no one's dream would be a sufficient basis for barging in to someone's home and excavating his property. Nor would we find law enforcement relying on superstition about avenging spirits, as they did in the following tale—a case that set a forensic precedent.

Forensic Use of Ghosts

The first trial that included fingerprint evidence in its crime reconstruction occurred in Argentina in 1892. A hysterical Francesca Rojas accused a man named Valasquez of murdering her two children with blows to the head. He protested his innocence, so the police chief made him lie all night next to the candle-lit corpses to shock him into a confession. This failed, as did a round of torture.

In the meantime, rumor had it that Ms. Rojas had a young lover who had said he would not marry her because of her children. This gave her a motive, so the chief turned to a rather unorthodox technique: he made ghostly sounds outside her home, as if the deceased children had returned to exact revenge. He hoped to frighten her into making a confession. This effort, too, advanced the case no further.

Juan Vucetich, who'd heard about recent theories about the utility of fingerprints for identification, had formulated a system for analyzing fingertip ridge patterns. He went over the crime scene and found what appeared to be a thumbprint in a spot of dried blood. He compared this pattern with both suspects and identified the mother as the person who had placed her thumb in blood. Thus, she was the killer. She confessed, was convicted, and was sentenced to life imprisonment.

Harbingers

Some ghosts have been documented returning to give information about their own deaths, as in our first tale above, or warning the living of imminent danger. In the Bible, the ghost of Samuel, conjured up by the Witch of Endor, makes several predictions that came true.

Another example is the ghost that reportedly haunts Aquia Creek Church outside of Fredericksburg, Virginia. The church, dating back to the mid-18th century, had an ominous beginning.

Built in 1751, it burned down this same year. A local undertaker with the fitting name of Mourning Richards rebuilt it in 1757. At some point during the early 19th century a woman was reportedly murdered in the church's center aisle and her body was hidden in the belfry. It remained there long enough to skeletonize, but the locks of blond hair found with the remains identified her. For nearly a century, her bloodstains remained visible on the flagstones. Thereafter, a cement floor covered them. However, her ghost popped up for at least one chilling tale.

Aquia Church

The man who tells it had served in the Army of Northern Virginia. He and another soldier had been scouting for Yankees near Fredericksburg. Around midnight, they came across the church and decided to stay there for the night, despite its reputation for being haunted. They fell asleep, but soon a noise woke them.

They listened, aware they could be caught, and heard footsteps coming slowly up the flagstone aisle. They wondered if it was Yankees but then heard a soft whistle that they recognized as an ancient Scottish fighting tune, "The Campbells are Coming." They gripped their guns, awaited this person's approach, but suddenly, there was only silence.

They remained tense, but after a while, they fell asleep again. Once more, the footsteps and whistling woke them, but this time they sounded closer. As they sat up, ready to confront whoever was in the church with them, the footsteps and whistling stopped.

They couldn't see anyone, so they settled back down. This happened yet again, but the third time, the noise began in the aisle right beside them. They were certain now that they'd see the culprit. They struck a match, but to their amazement, no one was there.

Fully awake now, they went to the door of the church just in time to hear a Yankee cavalry patrol riding up the road. With just moments to spare, they mounted their horses and escaped. They believed they owed their lives to the warning they received from the whistling ghost of Aquia Church, who would not let them sleep.

More recently, John Fuller's account in *The Ghost of Flight 401* had testimonial corroboration from a range of witnesses. In 1972, Eastern Airlines Flight 401 went down in the Florida Everglades. Everyone on board was killed, including Captain Bob Loft and second officer Dan Repo. Loft died during the rescue operation and Repo about thirty hours later. Repo had confessed that they'd made a mistake attempting to work on a mechanical problem while the flight lost altitude.

Some of the L-1011 jumbo jet's parts were salvageable, so Eastern decided to use them in other planes. It wasn't long before crewmembers on these flights starting seeing what they believed were specters. People seemed to appear from out of nowhere, especially in inappropriate places. Some crewmembers who had known Loft and Repo claimed that they were among these apparitions.

Eastern's management heard about it, but the company ignored the reports. Still, the reports continued, and passengers, too, claimed to see the phantom manifestations. Repo appeared most often, and he seemed to have protective intent. One day, some reports said, a flight attendant watched a man fix an oven that had an overloaded circuit. He finished and left. But then another mechanic arrived to do the work. The attendant told him that it was done.

"That can't be," he said, "I'm the only mechanic assigned to this plane."

Someone showed the attendant a photo of Repo and she identified him as the oven fixer.

Repo was often seen sitting in the cockpit or reflected in a window, and he seemed most concerned about safety. One flight inspector said that as he began his routine, Repo appeared near him to assure him that it had already been taken care of. Repo also reportedly warned a mechanic about a faulty circuit, which proved to be true, and gave an attendant a heads-up about a fire. Another problem that the apparition pointed out arose in a hydraulic system.

175

However, not all harbingers are benign.

Debbie Downer

The story has roots in a folktale from Red River (now Adams), Tennessee, known as the Bell Witch. There are several versions to this tale, but like the Blair Witch, it's about a marauding spirit out to do harm. For three years during the early part of the 19th century, many people (including President Andrew Jackson) reportedly observed what the Bell Witch could do. How much of it is true is anyone's guess, but this case is sometimes cited as evidence that ghosts can do some real harm.

In 1817, John Bell, 68, had a large tract of farmland overlooking the Red River. In December, something began pounding on the back door late at night after everyone was in bed. Bell would open the door, but no one was ever there. He and his seven children tried to keep watch, but they never caught the perpetrator. The pounding continued for another five months before the entity came inside.

The children heard sounds in their rooms like furniture being moved, chains dragging, and rocks hitting the roof. Sometimes the covers were pulled off someone who was asleep. They tried an exorcism, but the spirit retaliated by dragging one child, young Betsy Bell, around by her hair.

Eventually, the spirit began to speak in a female voice. She said she was a former resident of the town, Kate Batts, and she hated John Bell. Soon a mysterious swelling appearing on the inside of his mouth. In 1819, he died.

The spirit also went after daughter Betsy, breaking up her engagement and physically harming her in a poltergeist-like manner. (Some modern theorists speculate that Betsy had been abused by her father and had reacted with telekinetic powers, enhanced by rage and hysteria.)

The reputation as a harbinger arises from some notions that the Bell Witch also predicted the Civil War, the end of slavery, and both world wars. Supposedly she predicted John Bell's exact death date, but records indicate that she was off by a month.

Revenge

In 2011 in Zimbabwe, there was a published report that the restless spirit of former shopkeeper, Givemore Katangana, had vented its anger on a man who allegedly killed him in a bid to boost his business interests in Mudzi. According to the lore, a "ngozi" of this type is appeased only after the accused's family meets its demands.

The spirit of the murdered man spoke through two sisters of the accused (who had fled the area), and during their trances they assumed male voices and traits. Dorcas and Lavender caused quite a stir in Nyakudika Village, as each time Givemore's spirit possessed them, they beat up and harassed their own relatives.

In a trance in which they removed most of their clothes, wept, and writhed like snakes, they provided the details of Givemore's story. He claimed to have been murdered and mutilated, and his genitals were removed for a juju ritual. He knew exactly where his remains had been buried and he offered to show the location. The killer, he said, owed compensation. In addition, the victim wanted his private parts back.

"I am now useless without my sex organs," this ghost said through one of the sisters, "while the accused has his."

As compensation, he wanted "12 beasts." Otherwise, he would haunt the family forever. A frightened relative admitted that the accused had done the deed, so the family agreed to pay the compensation.

The Red Velvet Swing

In 1906, in what was dubbed the "Crime of the Century," Harry Thaw shot famed architect Stanford White in public at Madison Square Garden. White had designed over fifty of some of the most magnificent buildings in America, including Madison Square Garden.

Thaw was wealthy and had married Evelyn Nesbit, the original model for the "Gibson Girl." But she had a history with White. Nesbit had come to New York at the age of 16 to become an actress and model and met White who quickly seduced the beautiful small-town girl—not the first young innocent upon which he had preyed. She became his mistress for three years, engaging in many of White's fantasies, including riding on a red velvet swing.

Evelyn Nesbit and Stanford White

Ever jealous, Thaw finally shot White. After two trials, Thaw was found not guilty by reason of insanity. The mental health testimony was rather unique, but contrary to reports on several ghost websites, no one in the courtroom stated that a ghost had made Thaw kill White. That report occurred in a different venue.

Harry Thaw

After Thaw's second trial a psychiatrist, Dr. Carl Wickland, affirmed Thaw's claim to insanity and said that he'd been possessed. Wickland's knew this because his wife, a medium, claimed that the spirit of a man named Johnson had confessed to forcing Thaw to kill Stanford White. The motive was revenge against White for his treatment and rejection of Johnson's pregnant daughter, who later committed suicide.

Thaw was incarcerated in an asylum for the criminally insane, while his mother continued to try to prove his sanity. In 1915, Thaw was found sane. In essence, he got away with outright murder.

It's no wonder, then, that Stanford White's ghost has been seen roaming through Madison Square Garden.

The ghost of White allegedly also visited the wife of Dr. Wickland, demanding whiskey. Her claims were substantiated by Dr. Wickland himself who had witnessed his wife possessed by the spirit who identified himself: "I'm Stanford White, damn you!" The spirit admitted to seducing numerous young women and said, through Mrs. Wickland, he understood the anger directed at him by their fathers, all the while continuing to demand his whiskey.

Harbingers apparently indicate that ghosts are not just willing to pass on important information—they want to tell us things of importance, such as who killed them.

Evil Legacies and Restless Souls

In West Bolden England, stands a reputedly haunted eatery, the Wheatsheaf Pub. The owners make the most of its creepy aura by holding spooky events there. One was a charity event involving psychics, and among them was Suzanne Hadwin, who believed that at least three-dozen restless spirits were present in the place. Eight of them, she indicated, were children.

Suzanne told reporters for Newcastle's *Evening Chronicle* that she had seen a child's apparition, which had inspired her to do research. She believed she was in contact with the ghost of a 6-year-old, Jessica Ann Hargreaves, who was strangled and raped in 1908.

"Jessica was communicating with me," she said. "She'd been strangled and raped. He cut her up and trampled on her in the cellar. He tried to get rid of the evidence and threw all her clothes and belongings in a big fireplace."

Apparently the spirit child had told Suzanne that her killer was still hurting her. In fact, he was there among the spirits and his name was Joseph Lawrence.

Supposedly, Lawrence had treated a number of children in the same manner as Jessica, getting rid of the evidence in like manner as well. So he was a serial killer. Suzanne said that his presence infected the atmosphere and nauseated her. She was also frightened.

"I felt like he was going to go for me at any minute," she stated.

To help Jessica, Suzanne spent two weeks releasing the spirits who were trapped there, finally forcing the killer to leave, too. She worked with an artistic channeler who used Suzanne's descriptions to produce sketches of Jessica and Lawrence. They also took pictures, capturing bright balls of light.

Suzanne managed to learn more about Lawrence's background. He'd been in his thirties when he died. He often wore grey clothing and had been a local worker. Because travelers to Scotland often stopped at the pub, it was easy for him to snatch children. However, Jessica had lived locally, and her father had suspected Lawrence in her disappearance. In fact, Jessica's father had killed Lawrence himself.

Suzanne asked the pub owners to search inside a wall that covered an area where a fireplace had been. There they found a lock of hair, part of a child's shoe, and torn material that appeared to have been from clothing. Suzanne said these had been Jessica's. The evidence seemed to confirm the story.

Some cases appear to have been solved simply because official sources have closed them. However, they continue to draw attention from people who think the facts were incorrectly interpreted or ignored. The acquittal of Lizzie Borden is one, as is Marilyn Monroe's "suicide." The murder of Nicole Brown Simpson remains unresolved, although O. J. Simpson was convicted in a civil court, and "psychic photographers" claim to have photographed the image of her face, along with that of Ronald Goldman, in the leaf patterns of trees in the yard of Nicole's former condo.

If it's possible to acquire information via paranormal tools, which can be independently verified against factual evidence, then perhaps some murder cases can be re-opened or even solved.

We tried this in Savannah, revisiting the murder of Danny Hansford. As you recall, antiques dealer and preservationist Jim Williams claimed he'd shot Danny in self-defense. As you'll also recall, some say that Danny's restless spirit continues to show up, and Katherine got a voice on tape ("This ain't Dee!") at his grave.

A friend, Rachael, set up an evening with Angus McCleod to go to the "Buzzard House." He said he would be bringing two psychics, one of who had reportedly had an experience with "Danny" at this very property. Ray Couch, founder of Southern Ghosts, had rolled into town and wanted to come (and admittedly was something of a closet psychic), so Carol, Ray, and Katherine joined Rachael, her friend Lindi, and Lindi's boyfriend Jay, to meet Angus at an El Cheapo gas station outside Savannah.

Angus, a lean man whose rugged face suggested he had deep knowledge that he'd share if we earned it, introduced himself. He then offered us all a choice between Gatorade and bananas, either of which would raise our potassium levels (supposedly conducive for attracting ghosts).

Libby, a slender woman with curly blonde hair nearly to her waist, arrived and introduced herself all around. Then everyone piled into cars to go to the destination. It was a lonely one-story ranch-type house on a very rough logging road, with dense woods in the back.

There we met Maureen, who owned the Buzzard House, and Sarah, the other psychic. Sarah, a brunette with the kind of nurturing brown eyes that instantly pull one closer, was dressed entirely in white—a white T-shirt and full skirt. As she stood in the night air, she seemed to shine. Maureen, slender and brunette, was matter-of-fact and quiet, but quite willing to offer the house for our purposes.

Lindi told us about two incidents that Maureen had experienced. One was that her young son claimed to have seen a long line of Native Americans (apparently from another dimension) emerge one day from the woods. The other was that she had heard a bump outside the house one evening and saw a deer standing on her lawn. The next morning, she found it lying on her porch, dead. The Buzzard House got its name from the fact that buzzards are often seen roosting on the left part of the roof.

Buzzard House

Katherine entered the kitchen to listen to Angus talk to Sarah. He had a deep, gravelly drawl that wrapped around his words as he delivered them like they were gifts. He said that Sarah was the psychic who had channeled Danny Hansford at this place.

"I often don't recall any of it," she said.

"Do you remember what it felt like?" Katherine asked. "His energy? Because he was supposedly a very active guy."

Sarah put her head down as if trying to access to this past memory. She seemed to subtly move into another state and her face relaxed. She cocked her right ear a little as if listening. "He's aware of you," She said. "Have you written about him?"

"Yes, I have," Katherine said. "Is he here now?"

Sarah nodded. "He wants you to know something." She listened again. "He needs people to know that he's innocent, that he wasn't…is it *conscious*? He wasn't conscious? He was always bad. People said he was bad, but he wasn't bad, he's saying, he was good."

Katherine was curious. "Has he spoken to me before?"

"Yes," Sarah affirmed. "He speaks to you a lot."

"Tell him I can't hear him."

"Yes, you can and you do. He's always with you. Are you writing about him?"

Katherine knew that she would be. This story was going into *Blood & Ghosts*, but perhaps in a form different from what she'd anticipated.

"He wants you to write about who he really is," Sarah said. "He's been misrepresented."

Katherine was doubtful. "OK, maybe I will, but how can I hear him? Is there something I can do?"

Sarah gestured by waving her right hand in a tight circle. "Mindless stuff. Walking, cleaning…just let him talk to you. Grab the first words you hear and trust them. Trust yourself." She listened, and then said, "You're trying too hard. That's what he's telling me."

Then "he" apparently started talking to her about a murder.

"You mean, Jim Williams murdering him?" Katherine asked.

"No, not him. Another boy."

Katherine wondered if Danny had been involved in a fatal sex ring, procuring boys or helping to abuse them. She thought of Elmer Wayne Henley, a young man Danny's age who had procured boys for Dean Corll to rape, torture and murder during the early 1970s. Ultimately, Henley had killed Corll, supposedly in self-defense, and had shown police where they had buried the bodies. Twenty-seven were exhumed (and a 28th victim within the past 6 months). Henley was still alive, serving a life term. It wouldn't have surprised her to learn that a man of means like Jim Williams was involved in a sex procurement operation.

"He said you'd understand when he said he was innocent," Sarah continued. "That he hadn't understood, and he'd been in an addictive relationship. He couldn't stop."

"Like Wayne?" Katherine asked, purposely using Henley's *middle* name.

Sarah shook her head and gestured in a "not so much" way. "He seems to be saying, yes, but not as much."

"Not as *many*?"

Sarah hesitated. "There's something…Candyland?"

Katherine was startled. Corll's nickname was… "Candy *Man*?"

Sarah shrugged. "I don't know. Maybe. But I see drugs, that it's about drugs, not candy."

Right again. It had been candy as a lure, and then drugs as the real candy.

"There's abuse," said Sarah. "Like he…or someone…was hogtied. For sexual purposes. He was hogtied. He was abused."

Katherine was still thinking about the murder he'd mentioned. "Can we solve this murder?"

Sarah shook her head. "I hear, 'it's for the ages.' I see bones."

"Bones? So, it *could* be solved. There are remains."

"I hear, 'a lot of work.' It would be a lot of work."

"Is there a name?"

"Marcus. I hear Marcus. He's here. A lot of them are here. There are lots of boys like this. They're all around us."

"There were more?"

Sarah paused to listen. "I get the number three."

Three. What did that mean? Danny had been shot three times. Three people had worked on Corll's procurement team. Supposedly, one story making the rounds was that Williams and two other men had initially tried to get rid of Danny's body. Or did he mean *he* had been involved in killing three other boys?

Katherine wondered if this was the leverage that Danny had exercised over Williams: He'd known about fatal sex trysts that Williams had orchestrated. Had he threatened to blow Williams' cover that night in Williams' home? Had Williams shot him to keep him quiet?

Sarah had her hands at her throat. "Something here. Choked? Was he choked? Yes."

"Like sexual asphyxia?"

"Yes. I get, 'yes.'" She nodded.

"Did he help to bury them?"

"There were a lot of boys. Different boys had different dirty jobs."

So, he wasn't saying if he'd buried anyone.

"I see files," Sarah said. "A lot of files." She looked at Katherine. " Do you have a lot of files?

"Yes." Katherine's office, as always, was a mess of files in many piles for each project. Files and files.

"He wants you to write his story."

Katherine snorted. She wasn't buying it. "I can't hear him. Why would he choose someone so limited?"

"He says you listen well. You do hear. You don't realize it. He looks over your shoulder when you write. He likes to do that."

"So, it's like automatic writing?"

"Yes, like that." She nodded. "He says it was addicting. You understand? He thinks you do."

"I agree that I'm the right person to describe the dynamics of these relationships," Katherine responded, "because I've studied them, but I'm not the right person to know if I'm getting *his* story right."

Sarah nodded. "Trust. Trust the words. That's what he's saying. Tune in."

Katherine told her about the EVP at his grave and asked, "Was he telling me that the Danny I knew from the stories isn't really him? This ain't D, as in Danny?"

Sarah wasn't sure. She said, "He's there beside you. He's over your left shoulder."

This gave Katherine a chill. Numerous mediums over the years had told her there was an agitated man over her left shoulder, talking to her.

Then Sarah said, "I'm getting six. The number six. Like he's been around for some time, like six weeks? Six months? I'm not sure."

"Six years." That was how long it had been since Katherine was at Danny's grave. She wondered if he'd followed her. That's when she'd first written about him as well. "How old were the boys? Younger than him?"

Sarah shook her head, but then went still. "Two. Two are younger."

"Has he met them over there?"

She smiled. "Yes. They're OK. They're fine."

"Then what does he want?"

Sarah listened. Haltingly, she said, "R-r-rest. He wants rest."

"And I can do that for him?"

"Tell the story. He wants it told. You can do that. He was told that he was bad by everyone, but he wasn't bad. Since childhood, he was abused. He was not loved. He was misunderstood. All he knew was violence. He was innocent. He didn't know anything else. He wants compassion. He was a pretty boy. You can see more in him. Sometimes he was treated tenderly."

"Yes, that's the addicting part," said Katherine. "That's how it's done. Meanness mixed with affection. That's classic master-slave stuff."

"Yes. He's saying yes. It was a difficult relationship, but he didn't know anything else. He had never been treated well. I'm getting something about a car, a Mustang. There are lots of boys around him, other boys. He wants you to know how, it was about…they would strangle them and bring them back. It felt like God."

"The control. I understand. It was powerful."

"Yes." Sarah nodded.

"So, he was powerless and then he was the one in power."

"Yes.

"And it went too far, and they died." Katherine knew this was like the Corll crew. She also realized that if Danny had been abused as a child, then moving into a difficult but addicting relationship with Williams would feel like home, like a life force rather than something awful. No matter how painful or disturbing, it can be very difficult for a person to exit from that feeling. In his mind, he'd had to do what he was told. As he put it, he was "not conscious."

Sarah had mentioned South Carolina several times. Angus, who had wandered in and out, speculated that there were missing boys from South Carolina. Someone mentioned that Williams had had dealings in South Carolina.

Sarah moved from where she was standing an inch or so to her left. "It's like this, he's saying. He's slightly different from the ones you know. It's similar, very close, but different."

"Should I seek out someone like you to help?" Katherine asked.

"He's saying you could use someone. But I'm not sure…if it's like me or… You don't need someone else," Sarah affirmed. "You should have more confidence in him helping you."

Sarah's assistance was needed in another room, where others were dealing with the dark spirit of what they believed was a pedophile. They were trying to send him from the dwelling. It was an odd juxtaposition—Danny describing his relationship with an older man who sexually used him and other boys, while others were squaring off in the same place with a nasty pedophile.

The next day, we went to Danny's grave and called Laine, a psychic in Maryland who had been sending remote viewing reports daily. We told Laine nothing except that we were at a grave and we wanted to know if she sensed the person anywhere nearby.

Grave of Danny Hansford

"It's a guy," she said, "and he was murdered. It wasn't a clean murder. It's more involved than I can pick up on. It's more than a husband killing a wife. It was retaliation. I think there was money involved. I don't think that was the main thing. The guy murdered was to keep him quiet. There's a lot of anger. They were lovers."

"He has an urgency to have something revealed," said Katherine, still trying to shield details.

"I feel him on your end. He's listening to your thoughts. *Slow down, slow down!* It's like he… he knew what he was doing, but he also *didn't* know what he was doing. He didn't know what would happen as a result. He didn't know it would cause as much pain as it did, but there's something else. There's something physically in this world that he wants help on. There's something he wants you to know about. I'm getting papers, records, things like that."

"Can they be found?" Katherine asked.

"He says yes, but my guide says no. My guide thinks they cannot be found. Now this guy is saying, 'It can be found, it can be found.' He says he can show you. He can take you there."

"Is it in the cabin?"

"I'm getting no." Then Laine seemed to be talking to him directly. "Are you going to take her there, take her and show her?" Then back to Katherine. "You need someone who can understand him. There's someone you know that can help. The woman who was with you. Was he talking to a woman the other night with you? He can tell *her*. He thinks that she can help. She can hear him the way I can. He says he can show her. I think he means that physically, he can take you two. He says it's not far from there, where you are. They're not in the city of Savannah, but they're not far."

"Are they buried somewhere?" Carol asked.

"I'm getting a big 'yes' on that," Laine affirmed. "Are they where you are now? No. He says they're buried somewhere."

"Did the guy who killed him bury them?" Carol asked.

"He thinks he did. I'm feeling like he did not. I'm getting a big yes from him, but he didn't see the guy bury them."

"Maybe the guy directed someone to bury them," Katherine suggested.

"I'm getting a big yes on this."

"Does he want revenge?"

"No, he wants justice."

"Is there anything else he really wants Katherine to know?" Carol asked.

"Yes, but I think it's going to have to wait. It's something he needs to show her. It's more involved than I'm going to be able to get into. I think he wants to tell you details to straighten things out. You know them one way, but he wants to explain that there are things that happened that you don't know about. He needs to explain them, but it's going to take a while."

More psychics weighed in over the next few days, affirming the tantalizing information that Danny had buried some papers that held the key to revealing the S&M ring that Williams allegedly ran. Katherine was all for finding it and digging it up. She pulled out a map of the area to try to pinpoint possibilities and asked each psychic if Danny could show her the location. If so, and there was something to find, it would provide genuine forensic validation of a channeled murder victim.

However, not a single psychic was able to supply the last piece of this intriguing puzzle. Without it, however, there was no validation of the story. Whatever proof that was buried—if it even existed—would stay buried.

For a final effort, Katherine went to her computer, just as Danny told her to do, but he didn't reveal anything through automatic writing, either. (She gave him another chance during the proofreading stage, but still got no results.)

If Danny Hansford had been involved in the murders of several boys, what a story it would have been! But without evidence, the tale of Danny's death remains a mystery. [Bones told this tale to McCrary and he agreed with her conclusion: "'Danny' had his chance. So did the psychics. I'm left with the impression that those involved said things already known or easy to make up, but could not deliver what would really count as evidence."

Haunted Prisons

Sometimes a haunting scares a person into a confession. Notorious gangster Al Capone was imprisoned for a year in Eastern State Penitentiary in northwest Philadelphia, Pennsylvania. There aren't many places like this anymore, and once the imposing stone structure that covered a city block had served its purpose and became too expensive to run, it finally closed. Although the prisoners were eventually moved out, a few apparently remained.

Eastern State Penitentiary

The prison was built over a period of ten years and opened for business in 1829. It was the most expensive building erected in the U.S. to that date, with its medieval thick walls, vaulted windows, arched corridors, and imposing guard towers. With a central hub—the Rotunda —seven cellblocks radiated out like spokes from a wheel, and became an architectural wonder that attracted international visitors. This design was imitated in many other places.

Each prisoner had a room with a toilet, running water and a skylight dubbed the "Eye of God," and they were allowed contact with only a guard or minister. When taken from their cells, they were hooded to avoid distractions from the business of humility and spiritual transformation. Supposedly, with nothing else to do but contemplate his crime, a prisoner would learn to hate it so much that he'd never again be tempted to do such a thing. Charles Dickens, on the other hand, viewed these methods as an ignorant "tampering with the mysteries of the brain" which could have been worse than torturing the body.

There were many "inducements" to remorse and repentance. An inmate might be confined to straitjackets, given an ice-cold bath, entombed in vermin-infested trenches, thrown into smaller cells, strapped overnight to a wall or belted into the "mad chair," a device intended for uncontrollable psychotic patients. Worse, he might get the Iron Gag, where the convict's hands were crossed over his chest and tied while a device was locked over his tongue that would torture him as he moved.

Eventually these practices gave way and the place became a bit more humane. The prisoners were allowed to mingle, develop skills in workshops, communicate with the outside world, and even form teams for sports. Still, they always had to return to their cold, dark cells.

Among the more notorious inmates was gangster Al Capone, sentenced to a year in May 1929, for illegally carrying concealed weapons. He was allowed to furnish his cell with a rug, an antique desk, a lamp, a radio, oil paintings, and an easy chair to make his stay there more pleasant. Even now, for tourists, the place is decked out the way he had it, and the contrast between his cell and the others is startling. He was even allowed to conduct business and make long-distance telephone calls from the warden's office. Nevertheless, isolation apparently got to him (as it did many others), for he began to complain of a ghostly visitor: one of the men who had been gunned down in the infamous St. Valentine's Day Massacre.

It's worth revisiting that incident to understand who might have been haunting him.

Seven men were waiting on the morning of February 14, 1929, in a red brick warehouse of the S-M-C Cartage Company on Chicago's North Side. This was during Prohibition, and they were expecting a load of bootleg whiskey. Three men wearing police uniforms and two dressed as civilians arrived in a police car and went inside. Residents of the neighborhood heard the sudden rattle of several machine guns, and after the police left, some people went inside the warehouse and found a bloody scene: the seven unarmed men lay on the floor, all shot in the back multiple times. The wall against which they had been lined up for assassination was a gory mess of blood spatter and bits of human flesh.

It came out that the victims were known associates of mobster George "Bugs" Moran, so it appeared to have been a gangster hit. Moran pointed the finger at Al Capone, while Capone, in Florida, pointed back at him. But as it became clear that the shooters had imitated police officers, it seemed obvious that the massacre had been part of a gang war. When investigators were eventually able to match a machine gun found in the home of one of Capone's hit men, this information clinched it. Evidently, it turned out, the victims had been lured to the warehouse by a call about a truck full of hijacked whiskey was coming in, and were then slaughtered.

The other inmates at Eastern State could hear Capone screaming at night for "Jimmy" to leave him alone. One of these victims, James Clark, had been Bugs Moran's brother-in-law. Having heard the details of the crime, they assumed that's who the ghost was.

Capone apparently continued to be haunted by this spirit even after his release, because his bodyguards later reported that they'd hear him begging the ghost to depart. Capone's valet reportedly saw this apparition for himself on one occasion. Capone believed that the spirit had followed him from Eastern State, although why it might have decided to appear to him there is unclear. Perhaps the conditions were right.

Some of the inmates went insane and many died in this building, from abuse, old age, illness, and inmate violence. Many staff members who work late have reported eerie sensations, the sound of footsteps in cells or corridors, strange laughter, and glimpses of fleeting things in the shape of humans that were not supposed to be there. Often they're darting into a cell. Of interest to us were the reports from staff of a dark figure in Cellblock 12 that walks the long, dank corridors or just stands still, exuding malevolence. Another phantom figure is often spotted in the guard tower, as if a conscientious guard just cannot leave his post.

The prison went through several renovations, including the addition in 1956 of a death row, remaining in use until 1972. It's estimated that over 80,000 inmates were processed through this prison. It now sits abandoned and crumbling, a National Historic Landmark open for tours, art exhibits, and a special month-long Halloween extravaganza.

Extreme Violence

If ever there were going to be a haunted prison, it would have to be a place like the New Mexico State Penitentiary near Santa Fe, where a vicious riot took place in 1980. People were not just killed but also tortured, dismembered, hanged, and burned to death. Several paranormal investigators have learned from former guards or current custodians about disembodied voices moaning through the cell blocks, apparitions of former convicts wandering the halls, the sound of a steel pipe (like those used to bludgeon men to death) being dropped to the floor, and the harsh clang of cell doors slamming when no one's around.

It was just before dawn on Saturday, February 2. Inmates took four guards by surprise, stripping and binding them. One fled, leaving his keys behind. The inmates used the uniforms to surprise eight more guards—fully half of the correctional staff—and soon took over the Control Center. They also freed 500 inmates into the corridors. For the next thirty-six hours, as gangs fought one another all over the facility, the instigators were in charge of the overcrowded facility.

Some inmates broke into the pharmacy and took a variety of drugs. Others entered the paint shop where they inhaled fumes from paint, paint thinner and glue. Some grabbed acetylene cutting torches from the plumbing shop and made their way to Cellblock 4.

The inmates housed here were in protective custody, labeled by guards as informants. For several hours, the rioters worked at gaining access. Finally, they cut through the protective grill, yelling "kill the snitches." These "execution squads" used the torches to burn through cell bars, and some threw flammable liquids inside to ignite their victims. Several were dragged from their cells, stabbed, bludgeoned, and burned. One inmate's head exploded when a blowtorch was applied. A few were strung up to hang and some were chopped apart or thrown down stairs.

During the violence, 33 inmates died and nearly 200 were injured. Seven of the 12 guards had been injured as well. A number of bodies were found at the foot of the stairs. By mid-afternoon on

Sunday, police and National Guard retook the penitentiary, ending the violence.

Now ghostly figures and noises are reported in this creepy place.

The Rock

Capone also shows up in another prison where he was a resident: Alcatraz. During the late 1850s, military prisoners were sent to this small island off the coast of San Francisco. They built the maximum-security prison there for the most incorrigible inmates. Besides Capone, among the most famous were "Machine Gun" Kelly and the "Bird Man of Alcatraz."

Alcatraz Island Circa 1859

There were special facilities to break down arrogant men. The Strip Cell was a pitch-black steel cell where prisoners were stripped naked and fed once a day. Five other isolation "holes" were slightly more luxurious, with a light bulb and sink.

Alcatraz was closed in 1963, due to the high cost of its maintenance, but it remains open for tours under the auspices of the National Park Service. The place has an edgy, spooky feel, so it's no surprise to learn that tales have circulated of hauntings. Despite the prison's monotony—or perhaps because of this—there were several desperate attempts to escape. Three men were shot in a utility corridor as they tried to run, and their ghosts reportedly stick around.

Cell 14D is one of the five solitary cells, which exudes a clammy cold to employee and visitor alike. One prisoner locked into 14D during the 1940s screamed that a creature was killing him. They found him the next day, strangled to death. He was seen shortly after his death, standing in a few lines.

Reportedly, Al Capone liked to play his banjo in the room where inmates showered. Sometimes, park rangers hear the sound of a banjo emanating from this area.

Ghost of a Serial Killer

News sources around the world carried the story on January 15, 2007, that the prison cell once occupied by serial killer Harold Shipman, number D336, is haunted—by Shipman's ghost. While it's not exactly a haunted crime scene (unless one considers suicide to be a crime), it's apparently a haunted criminal.

The problem was brought to the attention of Wakefield Prison authorities by another killer, Roy Whitting, who occupied the cell after Shipman hanged himself on January 13, 2004. He claimed that he could not sleep in the cell and the problem was growing worse. According to the *London Mirror*, Whiting was hearing things that made him believe that Shipman's spirit was in the cell with him.

Although prison officials believe the "supernatural stirrings" were nothing more than other prisoners trying to goad Whiting, he insisted it was a genuine ghost. He was so certain about the haunting that he told his psychiatrist and the prison staff, and demanded that the governor ensure that he be moved to a different cell.

Ghost or prank, Whiting might just be trying to deflect a guilty conscience. The 47-year-old pedophile was convicted of murdering Sarah Payne, 8, on July 1, 2000. She had been playing outside her grandparents' home when he came upon her and kidnapped her. After killing her, he dumped her body in a field, where it was found more than two weeks later. But Whiting left fibers forensically linked to his van on the body, and for his crime he received a life sentence.

Prior to moving into D336 in "monster mansion," Whiting had been in a segregation cell. Once he was in his permanent cell, he apparently learned from others that it was bad luck, and being a sex offender, he became the target of pranks. Someone once left a noose in his cell for him to find.

However, Shipman was not the only prisoner to have ended his life in that same cell. Jasbir Singh Rai, only 32, preceded him, hanging himself there in April 1987. Shipman had given no outward sign of depression, so when he was found dead officials were surprised. It later came out that he'd planned to kill himself ever since he'd started serving his fifteen life sentences for killing several hundred patients. He'd even recorded his intent in his prison diary, plotting to ensure that his wife received his full pension.

Whiting claimed that as the third anniversary of Shipman's suicide approached, the eerie noises increased. As he got less sleep, he became more erratic in his behavior and neglectful of his clothing and personal hygiene. He *looked* like a haunted soul.

The Farm

When C. Murray Henderson was warden at Louisiana State Penitentiary (Angola), he allowed a brutal system of sexual slavery to develop among the inmates. It's little wonder that he feared dying in this "Alcatraz of the South" when he later received a fifty-year sentence for the attempted murder of his wife. To Henderson, the 18,000-acre plantation-penitentiary, with its 5,000-plus prisoners, was a hellhole.

Purchased with profits from the slave trade, the land is bordered on three sides by the Mississippi River. The facility opened as a prison in 1901. Fifty years later, it was called the worst prison in America. In 2004 reporter Paul Harris said "Unsurprisingly, Angola has always been famed for brutality, riots, escape and murder."

The prison burial ground, reputed to be haunted, is Point Lookout Cemetery. It contains the remains of the forgotten. A flood destroyed the first cemetery and the second one, with 330 graves, filled up quickly. Point Lookout II opened in the mid-1990s, with 700 gravesites.

More than one inmate claims to be haunted nightly by the ghost of his victim.

Spiritual, In More Ways Than One

The architectural style of Mansfield Reformatory in Mansfield, Ohio, was inspired by German castles. The architect hoped it would uplift the spirits of the boys sent there. Built in 1896, it closed in 1990. Rumors sprang up that spirits of boys that had been tortured roam the abandoned halls.

The accidental shooting of the warden's wife, Helen Glattke, inspired one story. People report smelling her rose perfume or feeling a rush of cold air in the administrative wing, where she and her husband lived. Other ghost stories surround the chapel, the infirmary, and the basement area. Reportedly, a 14-year-old was beaten to death in the basement. Psychics also report seeing the apparition of a young woman, possibly a nurse.

Mansfield Reformatory

Haunted Murder Items

Bundy's Chair

Theodore Robert "Ted" Bundy was one of the country's most notorious serial killers. Just before his execution in 1989, he confessed to killing at least 30 young women in six states. He was educated and charming, and used every trick he could think of to prevent his execution in Florida's electric chair. However, no effort saved him, not even his promise to provide more victims' names and locations.

In 2001, a guard from the state prison where Bundy had spent his final days told a reporter that shortly after Bundy was put to death, several guards saw him on a number of occasions sitting casually in the electric chair. The guard described Bundy's expression—a "knowing smile"—as if he knew something they didn't. If a guard attempted to approach him, he'd disappear. The guard telling the story said that there were so many sightings at one point that the warden couldn't find a guard willing to enter the room alone.

Bundy also showed up around his holding cell. To some guards, he'd say, "Well, I beat all of you, didn't I?"

Gacy's Curse

A news item in November 2005 featured Nikki Stone, a musician who purchased a painting of "Pogo the Clown" done by infamous killer John Wayne Gacy. Gacy had murdered 33 young men and kept the remains of 29 of them beneath his house. According to Stone, once he acquired the painting for $3000, he was hit with a load of bad luck. His dog died, his mother was diagnosed with cancer, and several associates who agreed to store the work experienced accidents or fires.

"I just want to be rid of it," Stone said in the *Boston Herald*. In the same article, Stewart noted that actor Johnny Depp had once acquired a Gacy painting, but had "developed a pathological fear of clowns and had unloaded the artwork."

The Gun With a Mind of Its Own

Dolph McCleish, of Monroe, Louisiana, collects firearms. In his collection is the historic Remington Model 8 rifle that Deputy Prentiss Oakley used during the ambush of Bonnie Parker and Clyde Barrow. Oakley shot Clyde and the bullets probably also hit Bonnie, as she sat next to Clyde in their car. McCleish said that that a friend, who had passed away, had willed him the gun. The man's widow claimed that it was "haunted." She explained that it would shoot by itself.

Shortly after getting the gun, McCleish decided to try it out. He loaded it and to his surprise, the rifle fired by itself. It scared him and he vowed to leave it alone.

Then a relative of the man who'd willed him the rifle showed up at his door and stated that the gun should have been given to him. McCleish handed it over.

Two weeks later, the relative returned and gave the rifle back without explanation. McCleish suspected that he'd been just as spooked by it.

Reverse Curse

Ned Heindel authored a book about Hexenkopf, an area in Williams Township in Pennsylvania in which stories of demons and witches flourished for a time. John George Hohman, who resided there during the 19th century, penned *Der Lange Verborgene Freund* (*The Long Lost Friend*), printed in 1820. It soon became a bible for occultists and faith healers.

Supposedly, those who possessed this book gained power and protection, but apparently that didn't work out for Nelson Rehmeyer over near York, Pennsylvania. It seems that a rival witch doctor, John Blymire, was feeling under the weather for quite a while, and had suffered a series of setbacks. He learned from another witch doctor that Rehmeyer was the cause. To gain relief, Blymire would have to burn Rehmeyer's copy of the Hohman book of spells, or get a lock of his hair and burn that.

Just after midnight on November 28, 1928, Blymire and two accomplices entered Rehmeyer's home and murdered him, hacked up his body, and burned it. They were arrested and tried. All three were convicted.

Bullets and Bricks

When smoothbore pistols and muskets were replaced in the late 18th century by rifled weapons, spent bullets acquired a distinct signature. The process of making grooves in rifles for more accurate projectiles meant that they would leave a mark on the softer metal of the bullet as it spun through the barrel. When bullets were then encased in cartridges, even more marks were made, helping investigators make a match between a bullet and a gun.

We've already mentioned the St. Valentine's Day Massacre of 1929. Recall that seven men were waiting that morning in a red brick warehouse on Chicago's North Side, at 2122 North Clark Street. Five men arrived and slaughtered them. The wall against which they had been lined up for the assassination was a gory mess.

St. Valentine's Day Massacre Scene

The shooters had left behind seventy cartridge casings and the weapons were identified as .45-caliber Thompson submachine guns. Since the police had such weapons, they had to be cleared.

This task fell to Calvin Goddard. With Charles Waite, he'd begun to acquire data from all known gun manufacturers to develop a comprehensive database. Together they'd catalogued the results of test fires from each type of gun. After Waite died in 1925, Goddard had resumed the work, and he was responsible for bringing the science of ballistics into its own.

With the invention of the comparison microscope by Goddard's partner, two objects could be laid side-by-side for high-powered comparative examination using reflective mirrors and lenses. Bullets could be laid out in such a way as to show whether there was a match in the markings that a gun would leave on them after they were fired from that gun.

When the seven bullet-ridden bodies were found in the Chicago warehouse, Goddard came from New York as an independent investigator and test-fired each of the eight machine guns owned by the Chicago police. He compared the results to evidence collected at the scene. No casings matched, which meant that someone had impersonated police officers. Eventually, ballistics analysis identified the perpetrators as members of Al Capone's gang. The success in this case inspired the country's first crime lab.

When the S-M-C Cartage building was torn down, souvenir collectors went to grab bricks. No one was thinking that perhaps they possessed residual paranormal energy. One man who picked up four bricks ended up with bad luck in fours: four divorces, a quadruple bypass, and four polyps that required surgery.

The Bloody Benders

While Kansas was still a frontier area being settled by immigrants, travelers passing through the southeastern part of the state found a warm welcome and roadside entertainment in the Bender family's log cabin. The Benders had arrived from Germany around 1870, and built their home between Thayer and Galesburg as a general store and way-station.

Daughter Katie posed as a spiritualist who claimed to summon ghosts and she had sufficient charm to learn a traveler's financial state. She could also persuade those with money on them to sit in a certain area for dinner or for a reading. Behind the ill-fated traveler hung a canvas curtain, and behind that stood Old Man Bender with a sledgehammer. He would deliver the fatal blow, while Ma Bender, Katie and John, Jr. removed the victim's money and dropped him down a trap door.

Someone was bound to notice, and when Dr. William York disappeared in 1873, his brother came looking for him. While at the house, he happened to see something once owned by his brother, so he went to the local sheriff.

The Benders abandoned the place before anyone could arrest them, and when a heavy rain showed the clear outline of several graves in their orchard, the entire area was dug up. Ten bodies were exhumed, including a child who'd been tossed into the grave alive and then crushed beneath her father's corpse.

This story swept the nation, and souvenir hunters took the Bender cabin apart, acquiring scraps of wood, nails, and anything that could be sold for high prices. Whatever remained was razed, and only a large hole was left where the house and store had been. The Benders were identified in various locations, north and south, but no sighting proved accurate.

The Search for Bodies in the Bender's Orchard

Ghosts of the victims showed up around the empty hole where the house had been, and reportedly, one can hear them shrieking or moaning in the dark. Some say the items removed from the house carried some of these spirits with them.

Séances With Serial Killers

The Mad Butcher

In September 1934, part of a woman's torso, with legs severed at the knees, washed up on the shore of Lake Erie in Cleveland, Ohio. A year later in the garbage-strewn area known as Kingsbury Run, two headless, mutilated male corpses were found with genitals removed. The younger one was identified as a small-time criminal, and the police dismissed his murder as his just desserts.

But then, early in 1936, the remains of a prostitute were found in a basket behind a butcher shop, and another decapitated male corpse turned up in Kingsbury Run, inspiring the Cleveland *Plain Dealer* to dub the killer "the Mad Butcher of Kingsbury Run." Two more mutilated bodies surfaced, making seven.

The city's Director of Safety was none other than Elliott Ness, former G-man and founder of the Untouchables. He assigned a dozen detectives to the case and burned down the slum from where many victims had come, but corpses continued to show up for two more years. By then the number had reached a dozen, but the killer eluded identification. Ness focused on one suspect, who then committed himself to a mental hospital and was never proven guilty.

Detective Peter Merlyo stayed on the case until his death in 1947, believing that the killer had actually murdered many more people than the official tally. He was certain that many of the bodies found during the 1920s in a place nicknamed "Murder Swamp," just outside New Castle, Pennsylvania, were victims of the Torso Killer's handiwork. The detective thought the killer was traveling by boxcar to elude law enforcement and to find victims in other places.

In 1925, three headless bodies turned up in Murder Swamp, a seemingly convenient place to dispose of them. Despite believing that murders could be linked via similar MO and similar terrain, the detective never solved these crimes.

Then, after the final murder in Cleveland associated with the Mad Butcher, more bodies turned up. In October 1939, the corpse of a young male surfaced in Murder Swamp, and then three dismembered bodies, one with carvings on his chest, were found in some boxcars that had come from Youngstown, Ohio, not far from Cleveland.

Pittsburgh had its own headless body, removed from one of the rivers, along with two human legs found some time later in another river that flowed through the city. Then came another headless corpse.

That these victims were all connected has never been proven, nor has the Mad Butcher (a.k.a., the Cleveland Torso Killer) ever been officially identified. But people in Cleveland preserve the tale, and some say the ghosts of victims show up in the places where they were found. Local folklore even suggests that the Mad Butcher still hunts, restless even in death.

Restless Killer

As the year 1950 drew to a close, ex-convict William "Cockeyed" Cook, in his black leather jacket and "hard luck" tattoos, went on a murder spree. Once abandoned by his father (who'd raised him and his motherless siblings in an abandoned mineshaft), this 21-year-old forced people to become his hostages.

Near Joplin, Cook hijacked a family in their car and made them drive him from one state to the next. Back in Missouri, when a police officer drove by, he panicked and shot the three children, the parents and their dog. Then he drove around with their corpses for a while before depositing them in an abandoned mineshaft (much like the one in which he was raised).

Still agitated, Cook forced a salesman to drive him to California, where he killed the man. Cook was unaware that a manhunt was underway for him across the Southwest. He kidnapped several other people and took two men hostage in Mexico, but the authorities recognized and grabbed him before he could harm anyone else.

Cook was convicted in Missouri of the murder of the family of five, but California got him for the salesman and executed him in the gas chamber on December 12, 1952. He was buried in an unmarked grave in the right rear area of Peace Church Cemetery in Jasper County, Missouri. Three years later his father was buried there as well.

One story has it that Cook was buried outside the boundaries of the sacred ground, in order not to disturb the spirits of the others.

Since it's now a run-down place, unkempt and rather deteriorated, with only 29 plots, it naturally has the reputation of being haunted. Supposedly a ghostly figure has been spotted over Cook's grave, along with moving lights and strange noises. Some people have approached the figure, only to see it vanish right in front of them.

Murder House

John Wayne Gacy was arrested in 1978 and charged with the murders of thirty-three young men, most of whom he had buried in the crawl space beneath his home. Gacy had lived with the stench of death for several years. After his arrest, he confessed but then pretended to have an alter personality, "John Hanley," who was responsible for the crimes. His attorneys offered a defense of insanity based on a compulsion to kill.

A number of psychologists and psychiatrists put Gacy through a battery of assessment instruments and came up with a variety of diagnoses. The overriding claim was that he had experienced an "irresistible impulse" when he killed each young man, and thanks to alcohol had either blacked out or lost his inhibitions to such an extent that he was unable to control himself. The jury convicted him.

John Wayne Gacy

While investigators searched for bodies, Gacy's house was literally torn apart. They looked from attic to basement, dug up the garage floor and excavated the yard ten feet down with a backhoe. When they finally decided that they'd found all of the remains they were going to find in that location, the place was a disaster. The decision was made to just level it.

Eventually the neighbors got over having this monster in their midst and pushed aside the images of the bodies being carried out. However, Gacy's former property did not recover, as if the ground itself was mourning its abuse. Reportedly the grass did not grow back, even after two or three summers had passed.

The property was acquired and the new owners built a house and changed the address. They wanted no more morbid tourists gawking at them. And for them, the grass grew and the scars healed, although some would say that the victims who were never identified still linger.

Killing Their Own

During the summer of 1991, a young woman in Gloucester, England, made an allegation of sexual abuse against her father and mother, Fred and Rosemary "Rose" West. But she was too frightened to press charges. However, social workers went to the home at 25 Cromwell Street. They spotted sexual items and recommended that the youngest child be removed. Apparently, Rose also prostituted herself via contacts made through magazine ads.

The children told an investigator that they once had a sister, Heather, who had disappeared seven years earlier, and their parents often threatened them with being buried under the patio "like Heather." Then another item surfaced: twenty years earlier, the couple had been arrested for kidnapping and raping another girl. She, too, had mentioned a threat regarding the backyard paving stones.

In 1994, the police decided to investigate beneath Fred West's patio. Soon after they started, Fred confessed to killing his 16-year-old daughter, Heather. The police found human remains—Heather's—but they also found another body.

Fred admitted that he'd killed two more girls—one of them pregnant—and buried them in the yard. When the police made plans to take up the floors, Fred conceded that they would find more bodies.

The remains of six more young women turned up, crammed into square graves under floors in the house. To his gruesome list, Fred added his first wife, his stepdaughter Charmaine, and two other women. While the remains of three of the four victims were found, Charmaine's murder was proven with forensic analysis to be attributable to Rose, so she, too, was arrested.

Fred conceded that he had not told the whole story, but rather than go to trial he committed suicide. Rose was charged with ten murders and convicted on all counts. She was given life in prison. There was plenty of evidence that the Wests had sexually tortured numerous young women before killing them.

On September 2001, documentary filmmaker David Monaghan insisted Fred might have murdered twenty more people. Fred had confessed this to a social worker, as well as on tape for an unaired program. Gloucestershire police said there was insufficient evidence to investigate Fred's statements and they wished to block any airing of them.

However, the documentary showed excerpts from West's taped interviews, along with excerpts from his home videos. In one clip, West mentions that when the police started to dig in his backyard, the spirits of his victims "came up into" him. He then felt them leaving and tried to stop them. He apparently liked the idea that they still "belonged" to him.

In October 1996, Gloucester City Council demolished 25 Cromwell Street, the "House of Horrors." Apparently, Fred's spirit wanders around the streets of Gloucester, perhaps looking for his missing home.

Bundy's Ghost

We mentioned that Bundy seems to like the electric chair, but his ghost has also been seen around the areas where he committed the murders that earned him two of his death sentences. He sometimes stands on the porch of the building in Tallahassee where he'd rented a room. Some mediums claim to have channeled him and one believes that he's now interested in redeeming himself. There has yet to be any report that he's actually offered information in a crime that helped the police.

In 2011, *The Puget Sound Trail* (the student paper of the University of Puget Sound) reported that Bundy shows up there, where he once attended classes. In what sounds more like a hoax in poor taste, the report states that the students like him and have even given him a new name, "Teddy the Friendly Ghost," as well as "Best Dead Friend Forever (BDFF)." Supposedly, he hugs them and accompanies them on late night walks.

By Ouija board, he resisted their pet names for him, as well as communicating his despair: "I. C.A.N.N.O.T. T.O.U.C.H. T.H.E.M. S.O. M.A.N.Y. T.O. K.I.L.L. A.N.D. I .C.A.N.N.O.T. T.O.U.C.H. T.H.E.M." said Bundy in a supposed interview, via the Board, with *The Trail.* "I.T. I.S. M.Y. H.E.L.L."

Apparently, male students are just as fond of him, calling him a "crazy guy to party with, especially if there are girls dancing.... Hands down the best thing I have ever seen at a UPS party."

In this same article, they quote Bundy as making plans to join Jeffrey Dahmer. "T.H.A.T.S. W.H.E.R.E. T.H.E. B.I.G. T.I.M.E. K.I.L.L.I.N.G. I.S." he said.

So much for his desire for redemption.

Ritual for Dahmer

Jeffery Dahmer

Speaking of Dahmer, the Wisconsin-based serial killer famed for his cannibalism, Chris Butler purchased Dahmer's former home in Bath, Ohio, where Dahmer murdered and dismembered his first of 17 victims in 1978. He also buried the remains in the woods nearby, close to where he had a cemetery for dead animals.

"Twenty-four hours after I first saw the place with my real estate agent, Greg Greco," Butler said, "he told me of the house's grisly provenance. He called to say we have a disclosure issue. 'I knew Jeffrey Dahmer had been in the area. ... And then they said there was a murder in the home. It was of significant notoriety, and we needed to disclose it."

"Now, I won't lie," said Butler. "There is a twisted kind of cachet attached to living in a house where a famous homicidal maniac kicked off his career."

Although Butler saw no ghosts, he decided to have a séance, anyway. "I'm not superstitious or a believer in the paranormal," he told a reporter, "but after months of people freaking out about where I was living, I did begin to wonder if there might be some leftover bad business in the place."

Plenty of ghost hunters had approached him about setting up an investigation there. He picked a team of females, who thought that Dahmer's birth date, May 21, would be ideal. They wired the place up with microphones, night-vision cameras, and digital recorders. Several mics were plugged into a computer. Everything was tested to ensure that it was working. Then they left the house for several hours.

After they returned, they checked everything. One of the cameras was off, although neither the battery nor the film had run out. All of the gear that had been set up near the crawlspace, where Dahmer had left the parts of his victim for a spell, had malfunctioned. The computer had a new sound file that would not open, and batteries on one camera had died long before they should have.

Essentially, the women decided they had not gotten results worth reporting. But Butler adds a final note: "One more thing… I had hidden a secret recorder in the house to see if I could catch someone sneaking back in to fiddle with the equipment. And in the middle of the hours of house ambience and the refrigerator cycling on and off and maybe a mouse or two, there was something." He described it merely, cryptically as, "a funny noise."

He put the house back on the market in 2012.

PFI - Linking Outside the Box

The Outlaw Jesse James

As we stated earlier, an exhumation can be a valuable tool for getting at the truth of an unclear or controversial incident. We described the exhumation of the remains from the grave of the outlaw Jesse James, using mt-DNA analysis. This case would be a good set up for a P.F.I. team, because Jesse's ghost is supposedly seen wandering around on the former James farm. Thus, we have a potential spirit communication, coupled with forensic science. Let's return to that investigation and add the paranormal part.

On June 29, 1902, James's remains had been disinterred from the James Farm and transferred to Mount Olivet Cemetery in Kearney.

Jesse James

In 1978, another excavation took place at Jesse's original burial. This dig unearthed a spent bullet and an assortment of small bone fragments, some being animal, and others left behind in the 1902 exhumation, as well as multiple hair strands. The hair and bullet went into the James museum, but the bone fragments were reburied in a plastic container.

So, imagine that we're at square one: there is controversy over who is actually buried in this grave. Before digging, we would start with EVP, as well as some night-vision cameras, and perhaps some acoustic enhancement software. If information was forthcoming about the identity of the man wandering the grounds and/or buried in the grave, it could be compared to what an exhumation and DNA analysis turn up.

The totality of the evidence confirmed that the remains were those of Jesse James.

The first task for such an investigation involves collecting all available documentation, which means looking into court records, old newspapers, books written on a person's life and death, pathologist reports, and other records. Once everything is legally in place, and family members or descendants are on board, the team leader determines which specializations will be required. In some cases, it's anthropology, archaeology, and possibly tool-mark or firearms experts. In a case with flesh on the bones, you need a pathologist, and if there's poison involved, you need toxicologists. For teeth examination, you need an odontologist (a forensic dental expert). All of this was done for the James investigation. We would add a paranormal investigator and possibly a skilled medium.

Let's now turn to a similar case for which nothing has yet been done...and for which we have paranormal potential. Here's how we'd approach it.

Immortal Explorer

From 1804 through 1806, Meriwether Lewis and William Clark charted a course of 4,000 miles each way across the North American continent. President Jefferson instructed them to keep a log of weather conditions and a thorough description of their route. They were to report on the customs and languages of the Indian tribes that they encountered and attempt to win their friendship. Their great feat was  to accomplish this perilous journey without losing a man.

211

Just three years later, on October 11, 1809, Meriwether Lewis, 35, was dead. At the time, he was governor of the Louisiana Territory and had been traveling to Washington with his unpublished journals in order to plead for the government to pay debts he'd incurred. He set out on September 4, 1809, in the company of his servant, Pernier, and became ill along the way. He rested for a time and left again on horseback September 29, accompanied by Major James Neelly, agent to the Chickasaw Indians.

They arrived at a footpath, the Natchez Trace, on October 8, but when two of their horses wandered off (because they weren't hobbled), Neelly went to find them while Lewis traveled on to the next white way-station. He arrived on October 10 at Grinder's Stand, where Mrs. Robert Grinder offered him lodging. This is where he died.

However, there is controversy over just *how* he died. A spirit seen around the monument that marks his grave today might indicate a restless soul looking for justice.

The three accounts of Lewis's death vary. In the first one, Mrs. Grinder reportedly told Major Neelly that Lewis had been acting in a "deranged" manner, and at 3:00 A.M., she heard two pistol shots. She and her servants found Lewis bleeding, with one pistol wound to the head and one beneath his breast. He was conscious and supposedly said to Pernier, "I have done the business my good Servant, give me some water." He lived only a short time after that and was buried there.

In another account, Mrs. Grinder said that Lewis had conversed with her before he died in a calm manner. There was nothing that would lead her to believe he was in a suicidal frame of mind. At some point after he retired, she heard a pistol go off in Lewis's lodgings, followed by a thump on the floor and "Oh, Lord." Then another pistol shot was heard. Moments later, Lewis knocked at her door and said, "O madam! Give me some water and heal my wounds."

She had watched through a chink as he groped his way to a tree and back to the house, where he tried to scrape water from a bucket.

After two hours, she screwed up the courage to check on him. He was in his bed but awake. He showed her where a bullet had entered his side and she could see a portion of his brain exposed. He begged her to use his rifle to finish him off. She refused, so he lasted two more hours in great pain before he finally died. Only moments later, Neelly arrived with one of the stray horses.

A third report on November 26, 1811, from Major Gilbert Russell, commander of Fort Pickering, claimed that Lewis killed himself in a fit of paranoia

Lewis's death was followed immediately by conspiracy theories around Tennessee, in part because it seemed incomprehensible that a man could shoot himself twice like that, as well as just let himself die a lingering death in great pain. Also, Mrs. Grinder's reported fear of Lewis was illogical, given the context of her life in the wilderness, amid highwaymen and marauding Indians.

Some historians believe that Lewis was murdered and that his death was pre-planned by those who wanted to rob him. In addition, there have been suggestions that he was assassinated, with Pernier's complicity.

All three recitals agree that Meriwether Lewis suffered two bullet wounds. All three are in accord that no one witnessed the firing of the weapons. In addition, the motive for his committing suicide is, inconsistent. It was unlikely that a seasoned scout would have forgotten to hobble horses in an area known for danger and thievery.

A team of scientists believes that the answer can be found in Lewis's bones. One might still be able to trace a bullet trajectory even through bone that has deteriorated. In 1996, an official coroner's inquest was convened in Lewis County to hear the sworn testimonies of historians and scientists. The nine-person jury concluded that an exhumation would be the best method to resolve the perplexing questions surrounding the death of such a prominent American.

Lewis is buried on Park Service land on the Natchez Trace Parkway in Lewis County, Tennessee. The monument was constructed in 1848. Visitors have reported a restless energy, including the noise of a water-dipper scraping an empty bucket and the words "so hard to die." In such a situation, if paranormal investigators could gather some data that could prove Lewis's continued existence, as well as any message he has, this could add weight to the effort to learn what happened to him.

For example, paranormal investigator Patty Wilson visited the Pennsylvania site of the massacre of ten Americans during the Revolutionary War each year on the anniversary for 18 years. On each visit she attempted to get EVP, and for 17 years she was stymied. Finally she got some of the most remarkable EVP ever recorded. It is what Sarah Estep would call "Class A."

First, Patty picked up a quick phrase in French, "*Parlez-vous Français*," easily translated as "Do you speak French?" the common language between the British, Native Americans, Canadians and frontier Americans.

Next she recorded a harsh, loud whisper: "*Yankees*," the derogatory bastardization by the Native Americans for "Anglais"— English. Then, at the site where ten men were tortured to death, the same voice ominously informs the PIs, "*Yankees...dead!*"

Perhaps there is a time limit on how long a spirit can remain at a place to pass on information, but it is clearly hundreds of years. Since Meriwether Lewis died after the Revolution, with the right paranormal investigators using the right techniques, valuable information might be gleaned.

During field research for his book, *Civil War Ghost Trails*, Mark was visiting Kennesaw Mountain Battlefield with Katherine and wife Carol. At a site where the fighting was so horrible that it was named, "The Dead Angle," Mark attempted to gather some EVP. He asked a Union soldier who'd fought there, "What was the fighting like?" He picked up two syllables in response, a short but highly descriptive summary of the soldier's view of the battle: "Murder."

Information gathering is the key to both forensic and paranormal investigations: different techniques are available for each and are mutually beneficial.

Local Mystery

This case began with vague reports about the spirit of a woman often seen in or around the Wells Fargo bank building on 54 West Broad Street in Bethlehem, Pennsylvania. There were enough stories about consistent sightings in this area to warrant research. Katherine found an article that described the building as a nightclub during the Depression era, called the Colonnade.

On November 10, 1949, former hostess Ruth Mickley, 31, was found dead in the basement of the nightclub. Around 6:00 A.M., a utility man found her body on a couch in the bar area known as the Rumpus Room.

Building Which Formally Housed The Colonnade

There were few leads, and a coroner's jury listened to testimony from the Colonnade's owner, a bandleader, a waitress, and three employees of Lehigh Surgical Steel. They decided that Mickley had been hit with a blunt instrument, but could not determine who had done it.

There was an investigation and several people were brought in for questioning and polygraph testing, but suddenly, the DA announced that the case was closed. It had been an accident, he stated. Mickley had fallen down the stairs and hit her head. He didn't explain how a woman who fell down the steps ended up on a couch.

Katherine took this information to the current coroner and he agreed that the investigation was incomplete. Just because identified suspects fail to pan out does not prove there are no suspects; it could be a flaw in the investigation or someone who killed Mickley and left, with no one the wiser.

We thought that Ruth Mickley was killed, possibly by someone in organized crime, and that the DA had been threatened or paid off. Clearly, her case had not been closed with proper procedures.

So, it might be the ghost of Ruth Mickley that shows up in several buildings on that street. Paranormalists might contribute to solving the mystery by trying to contact her.

215

PFI: What Lies Ahead

Should forensic and paranormal investigations come together, the P.F.I. (not to be confused with CSI) team of the future could include scientists, forensic investigators, psychologists, ghost hunters, verified mediums, and even spirits of the dead. In addition to the standard forensic equipment, equipment from the ghost-hunting world would be utilized.

Every week, several forensic magazines list new products that are in development or that have proven themselves in the field. For example, a team of faculty members and students, in partnership with Aneval, Inc., a chemical consulting firm, and Executive Forensics, LLC, an investigation company, have improved latent fingerprint development with a revolutionary superglue-dye blend, fluorescent cyanoacrylage.

Standard fingerprint retrieval uses vapors from superglue to adhere to fingerprint residue and requires an additional dye stain for prints to be viewed clearly. Because fluorescent cyanoacrylage combines superglue and dye, the product can be applied in one step, saving time and money.

Portable analyzers, the increased ability to get fingerprints or "touch DNA" from previously inaccessible areas, and new scanning technologies can all transfer to ghost hunting when the equipment becomes available.

Also, a new development in photography could be useful. Australian researchers found that adding infrared light technology to existing cameras can detect blood that someone has tried to hide under a layer of paint. Infrared, it turns out, is better than regular light at penetrating paint.

Another example comes from an episode of CSI. The forensic team on the show used "acoustic archeology" that could translate human sounds that had been absorbed into physical objects, like clay. This relied on the science of interferometry, which combines two or more data input points to deliver a higher resolution manifestation, i.e., two energy waves that coincide to amplify each other.

The components for the receiving device involve a light source (such as a laser), a detector, two mirrors and a semi-transparent mirror. In simple terms, the laser pulse heats the acoustic waves to amplify them and the transducer converts them for perception by the human ear.

216

Since this technology has been used in sacred sites like Stonehenge, it offers something to paranormal investigation today. The same can be said for new forensic technologies in alternate lighting, scanning electron evaluations, digital identification, acoustics, and voice amplification.

Paranormalists are inventing new devices as well. Researcher Mike Collette has invented a "Paranormal Energy Object Imprint Capture Device" for reading residual energy from catastrophic events imprinted on objects once in the environment of the event. He is currently experimenting on parts from crashed airplanes. This is indicative of where the field of paranormal research is headed. If he is successful, what are the implications for using his device on a murder weapon, a victim's clothing, or items from a terrorist attack?

Gary Galka, an electrical engineer, has developed some instruments in response to the tragic death of his oldest daughter. Shortly after Melissa Galka died in a car crash, the family began experiencing seemingly inexplicable events in their home: the doorbell ringing on its own, family members being touched by an unseen being, the television changing channels, and lights going on and off. Often the whole family would feel as if someone else had entered a room with them; they would hear their names being called and experience the sensation that someone had kissed them on the forehead.

Gary developed the Mel Meter (named after his daughter), which combines several anomaly-detecting devices. His most interesting development is the RT-EVP recorder with which he might achieve real-time, two-way communication with a spirit.

With the advent of the smart phone, a number of "ghost hunting" apps are available for download. They use the smart phone's already existing technology, such as gravitational orientation and electromagnetic sensitivity, to determine anomalies in the surrounding environment. Combine these with the built-in camera, video recorder, and audio recorder and you have a rudimentary paranormal investigation kit that fits in your pocket and travels with you. You can even get an app for a portable flashlight.

There are thousands of recorded cases of death premonitions, also known as a form of precognition, or knowing when something is about to happen. There are several documented from the three-day Battle of Gettysburg alone, and scores more from the Civil War.

Scientist Dean Radin was conducting an experiment with computerized random number generators when the mass tragedy on 9-11 occurred. When he got back to his data he realized that between 6:00 and 8:00 on the morning of September 11, 2001, all the random numbers were skewed. This indicated to him that some huge undefined energy was operating *prior* to the event—lots of people somehow *knew* something big was about to happen. Add to this the dozens of people who cancelled their trips on the flights that went down and you have the tip of the iceberg when it comes to the potential for premonition and precognition.

The question certainly arises: Using paranormal means within a scientific framework, could a crime be predicted? Might there be a time when paranormal information could be used—even welcomed—into a forensic investigation? Might we be able to use current forensics to make spirits more accessible and easier to understand? Might more testimony involving spirit activity be allowed into court? Police are already using predictive analytics on computers to try to capture the results of intuition. If we could include genuine precognition, the accuracy rate might improve.

Extra-sensory perception (ESP) is already a proven human phenomenon, studied and tested in scientific laboratories at such prestigious universities as Princeton, Stanford, and Duke, as well as institutes like the Monroe Institute in Virginia, the Institute for Noetic Sciences in California, and the Edgar Cayce Association for Research and Enlightenment. The era of card guessing is over.

Scientists such as Dean Radin and Rupert Sheldrake have published books on phenomena of how humans have uncanny abilities to know and affect things in their environment. The United States government funded (and may still be clandestinely funding) programs in which participants were able to effectively remote view.

It was once the case that law enforcement resisted the use of fingerprints, and at one time, biometric evidence like DNA analysis was considered fantasy. Thanks to forward-thinkers, both are now primary tools in crime solving and prosecution of criminals. Couldn't paranormally obtained evidence be thought of in the same light: a crime-solving tool just waiting for a breakthrough to affirm its usefulness and allow it into the courtroom?

No doubt there will be some setbacks. When DNA evidence was first introduced, the collecting of samples was prone to mishandling and potential corruption, the early databases were small, and juries had difficulty understanding the science behind it. In addition, mistakes were made in testimony. Paranormalists can learn from these issues in the forensic arena to improve their science and record keeping and thereby garner increased legitimacy.

A look back at some classic crime literature sheds light on how forensic science and paranormal investigating can easily dwell together.

Let's take the legendary fictional investigator, Sherlock Holmes. His hallmarks were observation, education, deduction, and inference. Although at times his conclusions seemed to come from left field, he would demonstrate with logic how he'd arrived at them, confirming the use of reason and keen observation. He became the model for many modern investigators, fictional and otherwise.

The author who gave life to Holmes was, of course, Sir Arthur Conan Doyle. As we all suspect, a great fictional character is merely a reflection of his or her creator. Thus, we can conclude, somewhat Holmes-like, that Sir Arthur had similar keen powers of observation and logical deduction (as did one of his most influential teachers, Dr. Joseph Bell). Interestingly enough, not only was Conan Doyle a writer and physician, but he was also a believer in spiritualism.

After enjoying a successful career as a mystery writer, and creating his signature character in 1886, Doyle began his interest in spiritualism by attending and participating in classic table-tipping séances at a friend's home. The rational "Sherlock Holmes" side of his character won out, however, and he remained unconvinced. But his natural curiosity kept him interested.

Then Conan Doyle suffered several family tragedies, including the deaths of his first wife and son, his brother, two brother-in-laws and two nephews. In the midst of the Great War in 1916, he began supporting Spiritualism, in part in an effort to contact the familiar dead. His son Kingsley had been killed at the Battle of the Somme. He reportedly contacted Doyle from the afterlife and encouraged him to continue his work.

Now a firm believer, Conan Doyle went on the lecture circuit around the world, an endeavor that was supported by those who had lost sons, fathers and brothers in the Great War and wished to be assured they lived on in another realm. Conan Doyle suffered setbacks when he accepted false evidence from fraudulent practitioners. Then when he and his wife failed rather spectacularly to contact their friend Harry Houdini's deceased mother, he and Houdini had a falling out.

Upon Conan Doyle's death in 1930, several mediums reported that he had contacted them, assuring that we lived on as spirits. (However, a forensic investigator would ask for better proof than the word of a medium.)

Conan Doyle's greatest character was once the inspiration and teacher for generations of crime scene investigators; perhaps Holmes's creator can be the same kind of inspiration to paranormal forensics investigators of the future.

Combining the best of both worlds, in the interest of advancing our knowledge and ability to close cases and enact justice, it's reasonable to view paranormal forensics (P.F.I.) as a discipline worth consideration. We hope that the stories we've told will encourage investigators of both persuasions to learn new tools. We'll continue our own collaborations and hope to hear more success stories.

Acknowledgments

Katherine and Mark would like to thank to those who assisted with information and support: Marilyn Bardsley, Rachael Bell, Deborah Blum, Traci Brasse, Brad Christman, Ray Couch, Laine Crosby, Scott Crownover, Dana DeVito, Rick Fisher, Zack Lysek, Gregg McCrary, Joe Pochron, Patty Wilson, The Lizzie Borden House and Staff, The "Buzzard House" Investigation Team, and especially our editor, Carol Nesbitt.

Katherine also wishes to thank Sally Keglovitz for proof reading the first draft, and for being such an enthusiastic fan of the project.

About the Authors

Dr. Katherine Ramsland has published more than 1,000 articles and 45 books, including *The Forensic Psychology of Criminal Minds*, *The Ivy League Killer*, *Psychopath*, *The Human Predator*, *Inside the Minds of Serial Killers*, and *The Mind of a Murderer*. She holds graduate degrees in forensic psychology, clinical psychology, criminal justice, and philosophy, and teaches forensic psychology and criminal justice at DeSales University in Pennsylvania. Ramsland has worked with prominent criminalists, coroners, detectives, and F.B.I. profilers. She speaks internationally about forensic psychology and serial murder, and has appeared on numerous documentaries, as well as *The Today Show*, *20/20*, *48 Hours*, *Larry King Live* and *E! True Hollywood Story*. She also writes a blog, Shadow Boxing, for *Psychology Today*.

Mark Nesbitt was a National Park Service Ranger/Historian for five years at Gettysburg before starting his own research and writing company. Since then he has published over fifteen books, including *Civil War Ghost Trails*, *The Ghost Hunters Field Guide: Gettysburg & Beyond*, and the national award-winning *Ghosts of Gettysburg* series. His stories have been seen on The History Channel, A&E, The Discovery Channel, The Travel Channel, Unsolved Mysteries, and numerous regional television shows and heard on Coast to Coast AM, and regional radio. In 1994, he created the commercially successful *Ghosts of Gettysburg Candlelight Walking Tours*, and in 2006, the *Ghosts of Fredericksburg Tours*.

Made in the USA
Charleston, SC
29 December 2012